Knowing Where to Draw the Line

Knowing Where to Draw the Line

Ethical and Legal Standards for Best Classroom Practice

Mary Ann Manos

Rowman & Littlefield Education
Lanham, Maryland • Toronto • Plymouth, UK
2007

Published in the United States of America
by Rowman & Littlefield Education
A Division of Rowman & Littlefield Publishers, Inc.
A wholly owned subsidiary of The Rowman & Littlefield Publishing Group, Inc.
4501 Forbes Boulevard, Suite 200, Lanham, Maryland 20706
www.rowmaneducation.com

Estover Road
Plymouth PL6 7PY
United Kingdom

British Library Cataloguing in Publication Information Available

Library of Congress Cataloging-in-Publication Data
Manos, Mary Ann, 1950–
  Knowing where to draw the line : ethical and legal standards for best classroom practice / Mary Ann Manos.
    p. cm.
  Includes bibliographical references and index.
  ISBN-13: 978-1-57886-618-2 (pbk. : alk. paper)
  ISBN-10: 1-57886-618-9 (pbk. : alk. paper)
  1. School discipline—Law and legislation—United States. 2. School discipline—United States. I. Title.
  KF4159.M36 2007
  344.73'075—dc22

                                                                2007017401

∞™ The paper used in this publication meets the minimum requirements of American National Standard for Information Sciences—Permanence of Paper for Printed Library Materials, ANSI/NISO Z39.48-1992.
Manufactured in the United States of America.

This effort goes to my beautiful, intelligent daughters, Molly and April, and to my precious grandchildren, Davy and Maureen. You are my greatest blessings. I thank God for you every day! Mom

Contents

Foreword: Education and the Law

A PRIMER FOR EDUCATION STUDENTS, OR "WHY SHOULD I TAKE A LAW COURSE AS PART OF MY EDUCATION TRAINING?"

You are in your final year, getting your education degree from an accredited school of education. You plan to make a career as a public school educator. With that goal, can you answer any of the following questions?

- What is a criminal background check?
- I have bad credit. Can that stop me from getting a teaching job?
- What if I lie on my school district job application? Can I get in trouble?
- Currently, I am in the navy reserves and have been offered a job as a guidance counselor at School District No. A. If I am called to active duty, do I have any special rights as a School District employee?
- During my probationary period as a teacher, can I join the union at my job?
- What is FMLA?
- As a student teacher, I am not subject to any laws about student records, correct?
- Can a school district fire a nontenured employee in the middle of that teacher's contract?

You may be unable to answer most of the questions, but ask yourself, "Why do I need to know the answers?" Why? Because you are preparing for and hope to have a career in one of the most highly regulated professions—public education. And, what you do not know (or know how to find out) might not kill you, as they say, but it will kill your dream—a career as a public educator.

With that background, the purpose of this introduction is to discuss why I, as an almost 30-year labor and employment lawyer, believe that a course on education and the law is crucial to any education school curriculum. Also, I have set forth a road map for how such education law course should be designed.

WHY AN "EDUCATION AND THE LAW" COURSE?

There are at least three professions that require a law course as part of the mandatory degree curriculum: business, medicine, and education. As previously stated, public education is one of the most highly regulated professions. Not only are there rules, regulations, and school board policies that an education employee must follow; but there are state, federal, and, in some cases, local laws that apply to educational employees, as well. And, like an understanding of student learning behavior, classroom management, or education theory and practice, a grasp of basic legal issues and concepts covering educators is essential to being a successful educational employee. Ignorance of the law is never an excuse for improper or unlawful behavior, but that ignorance can have extremely harmful repercussions for an educational employee—loss of license, livelihood, and even liberty.

I strongly believe an education law course should be a mandatory part of every education degree program. And, these are my reasons.

Over the years, I have made numerous presentations to education students about their rights as education students and their first years as educators. I continue to be amazed and concerned by education students' lack of understanding of educational legal issues that could affect them for years to come. Education students must understand that decisions they make as students or before becoming public educators can adversely impact their ability to get a job in education. In addition, those same students must understand that decisions made during their early years of employment can adversely impact their ability to keep their job. This point must be taught and cultivated as soon as possible; thus the need for a mandatory education law course.

Schools of education must prepare the student not only for the challenges of teaching, counseling, or providing other educational services but also must prepare those students for the pitfalls and challenges they will face as educational employees. This preparation allows for a "career" in education, while the former prepares the individual only for a "job" in education.

Each year, education school graduates go into an unknown territory called a "workplace." In that "workplace," they are expected to know and abide by rules developed by others. Some of those education school graduates do not believe that the laws or rules apply to them, while others frequently do not apply common sense to their behavior both in and outside the workplace. In most cases, this will be graduate's first job in a real and regulated workplace—a fact that adds to the significance of an education law course. As an education law attorney who has represented numerous educational employees who have found themselves in employment- or career-ending difficulties,

I cannot overstate the importance of an education law course as a requirement for graduation. Legal issues in education can no longer be relegated to a passing remark in class or to a one- or two-hour presentation that not all students are required to attend. The failure to make such a class, especially as described in this essay, a graduation requirement seriously endangers the education student's ability to make a career in public education. Schools of education must address this need, just as they have addressed the rise of technology in education. The legal issues that face educational employees are not going away. In fact, they will continue to increase as public dissatisfaction with public education continues. Most education schools have a stated mission: to prepare their students to be educators. That preparedness must not ignore the legal issues that confront education students and employees.

WHAT SHOULD SUCH AN EDUCATION LAW COURSE LOOK LIKE?

In teacher education schools, an education law course curriculum should include (a) sections on the state School Code; (b) the powers of a board of education; (c) how to deal with administrative agencies, such as the State Board of Education, the Department of Children and Family Services (DCFS), the Teachers Retirement System (TRS), and regional superintendents' offices; (d) laws that affect an individual's ability to get a job as an educator and to keep that job; (e) the rights and obligations of an educational employee, including applicable criminal laws; (f) an understanding of due process; (g) the rights and obligations of student teachers; (h) the rights and privileges of students and their parents; (i) information on planning for the future, including employee rights related to retirement; and (j) the ethics of being a public educator. There may be other topics appropriately included in such an education law curriculum, but, in my view, these subjects are required topics for an effective education law course.

The suggested curriculum topics are crucial to any student seeking to be an education employee, whether the educational employer is public or private. The curriculum should not be designed to evoke fear of the education profession. Rather, any education law course must be threaded with the practical wisdom and common sense needed in the education profession. The course must be a foundational piece to an education school program's "survive and thrive in the educational workplace setting" curriculum that truly prepares an education student for the real world. Moreover, it is critical that any education student know how to seek advice and assistance from others to resolve a workplace problem, another essential element of the education law course curriculum.

And, while educators may not be dismissed just because they are unwed single parents, or have their paychecks garnished because of their sexual orientation, they still are subject to employment standards and applicable laws regarding morality, good character, and the perceived "best interest of the school district." Under the Illinois School Code, teachers may be dismissed or have their teaching certification revoked or suspended because of "unprofessional conduct" or other forms of inappropriate conduct. Furthermore, there are numerous administrative rules and court decisions that govern an educational employee's behavior, conduct, and rights. To be successful, education school graduates must know of these expectations and how, if necessary, to adjust their conduct and behavior to meet those expectations. Again, the value of a mandatory education law course to inform education students of these requirements and potential employment perils cannot be overestimated or ignored.

Most important, a mandatory education law course must be a part of the overall education school curriculum and must not be taught in a vacuum. In many instances, the education law course will reinforce the importance of things taught in those other classes and learned during student teaching. For example, the "classroom management" class has a direct relationship to laws and policies related to child abuse, teacher evaluation, parental complaints, and student rights related to discipline. Similarly, technology and its uses are increasingly important parts of the education school curriculum and an essential part of how children are now taught. However, technology and computers in the educational workplace raise many employment-related problems, including possible criminal, employment, or constitutional law issues. An education school graduate must be aware of those possible criminal, employment, or constitutional law issues, how they arise, and how to avoid any adverse employment and life consequences.

In addition, the education law curriculum can inform the students who are the "players" in the legal system and how that system works as it relates to educational employees. Educational employees are continuously in the public eye and believed by many to be "public property," with diminished privacy rights. Perceptions of an educator become reality—whether good or bad. And, protection of personal privacy rights may be dependent on what is learned in such an education law course.

Finally, not only must the education law course teach prospective educational employees about legal rights and obligations, but it must instruct the students on available resources, options, and strategies they can use when dealing with legal issues. Basic principles such as the importance and legal significance of employment contracts; the importance of maintaining and reviewing important employment documents, such as handbooks and policies; and the need to understand any collective bargaining agreements or insurance policies and benefits are important parts of what an educational employee needs to know and learn from an education law course. Moreover, it is important for this course to instruct the student in how to avoid conduct that can lead to employment problems. Clearly, the primary goals of the mandatory education law course are to prevent employment problems and to train students in how to deal with such problems if they arise.

WHO SHOULD TEACH THE EDUCATION LAW COURSE?

The final part of the course design is who should teach the education law program I have described. First, the course instructor should be an attorney; however, the presenters and instructors should not be limited to attorneys. To bring a real-life flavor to the education law course, instructors should include professionals from the various education-based agencies that make legal decisions that affect educational employees; representatives from both educational employers and unions; and both newly employed and experienced employees. Additionally, instructors from other education courses, such as classroom management or student teacher supervisors, should present in the education law course.

Second, it is my opinion that the success of the education law course will depend not only on the students but on the diverse and practical views the teaching faculty bring to the course curriculum. Such diversity demonstrates to the student how decisions can have different interpretations and consequences and trains the student in how to weigh behavior not only as it currently affects that student as an employee but for the future implications of behavior in the educational workplace setting.

In conclusion, I believe an education law course must be part of each education school's mandatory curriculum. Schools of education cannot be ivory towers of theory. Rather, such schools must continue to function in the real world of educational work institutions—a world with many hazards that must be faced and that education students must be prepared to confront. Unfortunately, such a course is a necessary evil given today's climate in public education. To provide such a mandatory education course in each education school program, with the diverse, pragmatic, broad-based, and common-sense approach I have urged, would serve a great purpose and aid each education school's mission—to prepare its students for careers as future educators of America.

Sandra Holman, Associate General Counsel
Illinois Education Association, IEA-NEA

CHAPTER 1

Professional Dispositions: Building a Professional Persona

Key Concepts

Licensure
Accrediting
Certification
Ethics
Normative
Core Values
Principles
Mores
Virtues
Dispositions
Incompetence
Insubordination
Immorality

This chapter will:

1. Introduce the reader to codes of ethics designed by several states, universities, and/or professional educational associations.
2. Identify the difference between a virtue statement and an ethics code.
3. Trace the process designed to enforce a code of ethics at the state level.
4. Discuss the professional dispositions described by the National Council for Accreditation of Teacher Education and their impact on schools of education.

WARNING! DO NOT SKIP THIS CHAPTER!

One Out of Every Five Teachers Will Be Either the Plaintiff, the Defendant, or a Grievant in an Action That Is Job Related[1]

What you know about your state ethics codes will impact your career in education. In truth, if educators spent time in understanding and utilizing codes of education, the entire remainder of this text would be unnecessary. Often, teachers, parents, and students simply do not know the impact of educational ethics codes upon daily classroom practice. Most practicing professionals do not routinely consult their codes of ethics.[2] Colleges of education simply do not offer their teachers preparation in education ethics, despite the requirements of other professional tracks, which routinely expect their graduates to have a minimum competency in the dynamics of ethical behavior and everyday practice. A habit of ignoring what you do not understand will not serve the reader well in the case of ethics codes. Practicing the ethics of just "getting by" is a poor choice when your actions may be reviewed in a court of law. Now is the time to become knowledgeable regarding professional behavior standards as outlined by your school district, state board of education, professional affiliations, and governmental mandates.

On the surface, ethical statements of professional behavior are quite general in nature. They may often reflect the unique perspective and specialty of educational organizations or the state agency that designed them. One might think ethics codes unnecessary, archaic, or of little relevance to present-day teaching practice. On the other hand, dusting off the code to analyze its relevance to the classroom in the twenty-first century is well worth the effort. In the past five years, many states have put sharp teeth into their established ethics codes and have put in place complaint processes, ethics officers (often attorneys on retainer to the district), review boards, hearing mandates, and potential certification restrictions that can lead to license revocation and/or suspension. Additionally, many schools of education are under accreditation pressure to provide clear and convincing proof that their teacher education candidates have displayed appropriate professional dispositions required in the classroom.[3] In the case of professional teaching ethics codes, what teachers don't know or have failed to understand can and will impact their success and longevity in the classroom.

WHAT IS AN ETHICS CODE?

Ethics codes are living and essential documents. A code of ethics is a series of statements that crafts an image of a professional role. It is a guidance system for everyday practice. A code of ethics serves as a foundation for daily practice. Begun in the late 1700s with the medical profession, ethics codes are official statements of expected professional behavior.

They describe the parameters of ethical behaviors—those practices a professional must or must not engage in. An ethics code is solely concerned with public acts made in the performance of professional roles. It is a shared framework for professional responsibility that affirms educators' commitment to the core values of our field.[4] In other words, an ethics code is a product that brings together our understanding of the common good (norms) in education.

Simply said, they help good people make tough choices.[5] They are altruistic in nature and benevolent in tone, and most are written as positive statements. Codes of ethics identify common issues and problems that may arise. They define a profession's common responsibility to the public to obey societal expectations of honest dealings and full disclosure.[6] They help teachers facing a difficult decision to find principles by which to discuss resolution options, as well as to verbalize the reasons and meanings behind each option. In analogy, a code of ethics serves much the same purpose as a rudder on a ship. They are implicit (present but unseen) in excellent teaching, yet guide the path of ethical practice minute-to-minute in the classroom.

An ethics code is quite distinct from other professional statements of intent. Neither a code of conduct (such as the Ten Commandments) nor an oath (such as the Hippocratic Oath for doctors), a code of ethics clearly verbalizes the values, norms, and mores of teaching. What are the core values, norms, mores, and principles of teaching? The following terms, working definitions, and examples come from actual codes of ethics formulated by educational organizations across the United States.

> Core values—*Commitments* by a profession that are consciously and knowingly embraced by its practitioners because they make a contribution to society. There maybe a difference between an educator's personal values and the core values of a profession.[7] For example, the Center for Creative Play writes, "Our organization *is committed* to promoting positive images of families and children, particularly those with special needs." [8]
>
> Norms—Conventions of a society; they are understandings that prescribe what one should do and *how one ought to act* for the betterment of society. For example, the American Library Association writes, "Librarians *must adhere* to the principles of due process and equality of opportunity in peer relationships and personnel actions."[9]
>
> Mores—A fixed, *binding custom* of a specific group or culture.[10] Statements of good, right, and proper behavior; ideas of how people should behave.[11] For example, the National Education Association writes, "Educators *shall not use professional relationships with students for private advantage*" [12]
>
> Principle—A general or *fundamental law*, a rule or code of conduct .[13] For example, from the Division for Early Childhood Code of Ethics, "We shall *give learners a fair chance* to succeed and diverse ways to demonstrate their competence." [14]

As the reader can discern, these terms may easily become blurred and homogenized, depending on the precision of the writer. Nonetheless, together they form the skeletal structure for all codes of ethics, regardless of the profession. The bottom line is that a code of ethics should define the standards of excellence for professional responsibility and accountability. The process of formulating, refining, and adhering to a code of ethics is a crucible experience for state boards of education, teaching associations, school administrators, and colleges of education.

Case in Point

The following statement is taken from the Council for Exceptional Children's Code of Ethics for Educators of Persons with Exceptionalities, Professional Standards (1993):

Members of the special education profession are responsible for upholding and advancing these principles. Members of the Council for Exceptional Children agree to judge and be judged by them in accordance with the sprit and provisions of this code.

- What commitments, norms, mores, or principles can you identify in this introductory statement by the CEC? See the entire code in the appendix to this text.

This one is from the National Education Association's Code of Ethics, first created in 1929 and revised in 1975:

The educator, believing in the worth and dignity of each human being, recognizes the supreme importance of the pursuit of truth, devotion to excellence, and the nurture of the democratic principles. Essential to these goals is the protection of freedom to learn and to teach and the guarantee of equal educational opportunity for all.

- In light of pervasive standardized testing, as required by the latest round of federal mandates, how much freedom to learn and to teach is available to the twenty-first-century educator? See the entire code in the appendix to this text.

And, finally, from the New York State Department of Education, State Board of Regents Code of Ethics for Teachers, Principle 6, adopted July 2002:

Teachers help students understand that knowledge is often complex and sometimes paradoxical. Educators are confidantes, mentors, and advocates for their students' growth and development. As models for youth and for the public, they embody intellectual honesty, diplomacy, tact, and fairness.

Talk It Over

- In your opinion, what does the term "intellectual honesty" mean?
- How would this ethical statement be applied when teaching controversial historical events such as colonization, slavery, or women's suffrage?
- How would this ethical statement be applied in light of modern scientific exploration, such as the human genome project, cellular cloning, or ethnic eugenics?
- Which is more important to successful teaching—honesty or tact?

DOES TEACHING REALLY NEED A CODE OF ETHICS?

A code of ethics is one hallmark of a true profession.[15] Teaching is considered by many to be a profession. In the working world, there are several levels of employment. They include the following: unskilled, semiskilled, skilled, semiprofessional (or paraprofessional, in education), and professional occupations.[16] Professional occupations are considered a lifelong work, established for the betterment of society. The establishment of an official code of ethics adhered to by practitioners is a significant prerequisite for the professionalism of an occupational group. It is one of the external hallmarks testifying to the claim that the group recognizes an obligation to society that transcends mere economic self-interest.[17]

What are the specific identifiers for professional status? They include the following:

1. The profession requires a high degree of general and systemized knowledge.
2. Entry entails a long period of specialized, intellectual training.
3. Practice is essentially intellectual in character.
4. The field is organized to provide a unique social service.
5. There are standards of entrance and exclusion.
6. The work entails a broad range of autonomy.
7. The profession enforces a professional code of ethics (the most important for this chapter).[18]

(The last characteristic will be looked at in much greater detail as this chapter describes twenty-first century efforts to police the nation's six-million-member teaching force.)

The keystone characteristics of professions include the notion that professionals are highly skilled and knowledgeable autonomous agents who act within the support and constraint of professional relationships. They act in ways that transcend immediate self-interest.[19] A code of ethics therefore becomes the bedrock foundation for teaching as a profession.

Teaching is in a unique position to claim professional status in that teachers assume a duty or obligation that goes beyond that of most other professions, other than the ministry. Doctors or lawyers have professional duties to improve the welfare of their patients but are not held to account for failing to improve the moral values and/or conduct of those they serve, as teachers and schools are.[20]

Professor David Carr, of the University of Edinburgh (2003), describes several ways of thinking about teaching as a profession.

1. *Educators serve as "cultural custodians."* Teachers are in the business of upholding a particular way of life, much like ministers or priests.
2. *Educators serve as caregivers.* Teaching is on the same level as child minding, nursing, or midwifery.
3. *Educators serve as social workers.* Teachers model the teacher-student relationship as personal therapists.

4. *Educators serve as classroom technicians.* The excessive state and federal controls on testing and curriculum have so limited teaching as to reduce teachers to technical tradesman (or semiskilled) status.
5. *Educators serve as high-level professionals.* Teaching is akin to doctors and lawyers in that all of these have developed a basis for self-regulation, which is necessary for achieving the ultimate professional status.
6. *Educators serve as business executives.* The process of school-choice alternatives has imposed a market economy on both failing and successful schools. Students are the consumers. Teachers are the salespeople.

Which role most closely matches the actual task of teaching? In truth, education is a mix of all of Carr's elements.

Teachers carry both legal and moral authority, by way of *modeling* moral behavior, to act in such a way as to lead youth in a positive and beneficial direction. Many education ethics codes include the description of teachers as holding a "public trust and responsibility that requires the highest ideals of professional service." Many states include some variant of the phrase "has been found to be found of high moral character" in the teacher licensure certificate. American civil and criminal courts have consistently held teachers to a higher standard than members of other professions because of the high privilege of working with the nation's youth.[21] Teachers are expected to guard their personal honor if they are to remain effective educators in the classroom.[22] No excuses can be given for those who transgress societal mandates or violate accepted professional or personal practices.

Case in Point

From the New York State of Education Department, State Board of Regents Code of Ethics for Teachers, adopted July 2002:

This code shall not be used as a basis for any employer and shall not be used by the State Board of Education Department as a basis for any . . . decisions pertaining to certification or employment in New York State.

The Florida Department of Education Code of Ethics of the Education Profession, section 6B-1.006-2, includes the following warning:

Violation of any of these principles shall subject the individual to revocation or suspension of the individual educator's certificate, or other penalties as provided by law.

Talk It Over

In your opinion, should ethics codes be used to identify clear "outliers" in the mainstream educational community and eliminate them from certified teaching positions?

- Why or why not?
- Could you agree to conduct yourself and your professional practice in compliance with either code of ethics?
- Which would you favor?

See the entire code in the appendix of this text.

WHAT IS MEANT BY "VIRTUE" STATEMENTS?

What is the true purpose of an education? Perhaps your answer included one of the big three reasons for attaining an education in the twenty-first century:

1. To get a good paying job.
2. To become a better citizen who will in turn construct a better society.
3. To be a more enlightened (educated) person.

The way you have answered that question will dictate your approach to ethics codes, as well as to classroom teaching. In fact, your answer reveals your greater philosophy of education. Virtue statements have to do with becoming an enlightened person. Although this volume does not attempt to explain forms of educational philosophy and how philosophy impacts daily classroom practice, we will look at the purpose of virtue statements in ethics codes

The history of developing moral and intellectual virtue statements begins quite early in pedagogical history. For Socrates, the purpose of education is not to refine one's persuasive abilities (rhetoric) or develop a marketable commodity or skill; rather, he believed that true education is to be regarded as an indispensable precondition to personal growth and individual moral development.[23] Later, Aristotle clearly delineated the difference between a vice and a virtue. Virtuous persons were those who exhibited characteristics worthy of being emulated. Persons who lived in a way that exemplified a "good life" were those who embodied virtue. They displayed behaviors that encouraged commonly acceptable social bonds and performed their functions in life with excellence.[24] Ethics codes based on virtue statements expect teachers to display certain character traits and frames of mind. Virtue statements expect educators to embody specific ideals for excellence in their personal practice. Teachers must develop a complex, internalized picture of educational professionalism, only lightly shaded by context. Simply said, teaching virtues are internally held, not externally dictated. It logically follows, then, that the education profession becomes a corporate display of individual personal characteristics. Virtue statements describe an inward, motivating force, rather than an outward target at which to aim. Such ethical virtues emphasize an internal locus of control, rather than an external locus of control. They describe an ethical ideal that is being built throughout the educational program as teachers develop, practice, and mature in their craft. Virtues exist at the intersection of (internal) personal excellence and (external) professional competence.

Case in Point

Many states have begun to describe teaching through the use of virtue statements. Illinois includes the following expectations for professional teachers in the Illinois Professional Teaching Standards:

> IL-PTS.3.F—The competent teacher understands personal cultural perspectives and biases and their effect on one's teaching.
>
> IL-PTS.3.J—The competent teacher uses cultural diversity and individual student experiences to enrich instruction.
>
> IL-PTS.3.N—The competent teacher demonstrates positive regard for individual students and their families regardless of culture, religion, gender, sexual orientation, and varying abilities.

Talk It Over

- How do the statements just presented describe internal characteristics, rather than external characteristics?
- Could these statements be used to judge whether a teacher is incompetent? How?
- Give an example from your own schooling experience of teacher competency or incompetence related to each statement.
- Can the qualities described in the first statement be measured?

WHY INCLUDE PROFESSIONAL ETHICS COURSES IN TEACHER PREPARATION PROGRAMS?

When do teacher candidates study educational ethics, and how do educational ethics directly impact professional practice? Teachers are the only professionals to emerge from their initial preparation (at the undergraduate level) lacking a course in the ethical and legal demands of professional practice in modern American schools. Most other professionals include a course in ethical or legal mandates and current case law. Examples include business ethics courses, medical ethics courses, and economics ethics; courses are also offered in engineering, the media, and journalism, as well as human service. On the other hand, most schools of education attempt to imbed ethics in low-level educational history courses. Many pre-service teachers were introduced to educational philosophy and ethical codes in very early (freshman-level) teacher education courses. The concept of ethical practice is soon forgotten or ignored, because the information never receives any emphasis from those the students consider to be most knowledgeable about what successful classroom practice requires—the professors. The study of educational ethics often is considered less valuable than the study of instructional strategies, content, lesson delivery, and disciplinary management. Other programs simply assume that their education majors will assimilate ethical and legal standards from methods courses.

One way colleges of education teach ethics, albeit on an implicit level, is through case studies that involve hypothetical situations meant to encourage moral and ethical thinking. Student reflection and discussion of the best path for professional practice in each hypothetical case is encouraged. Although a case study or hypothetical-situation discussion is a common strategy in ethics education, as seen in Lawrence Kohlberg's work, *Moral Steps and Moralization* (1976), the final conclusion must never be that one should do whatever one thinks best in each situation. What one thinks best may indeed cross legal, professional, and ethical boundaries. The end result? Many colleges of education include ethics studies at the precise time when it will have the least impact on the educator's professional preparation.

HOW IMPORTANT IS A MATURE, INFORMED KNOWLEDGE OF TEACHING ETHICS FOR THE PROFESSIONAL TEACHER?

Experienced voices sound loudly:

Your belief system will drive why you teach. As a teacher—your responsibility for your action is ever keen. What you say and do has profound implication—lives are in the balance. Your very approach [to the act of teaching] manifests what you are. The obverse is also true; if you reflect on nothing and stand for nothing and value nothing, then the quality of your lessons will exhibit emptiness. [25]

In what ways do I benefit or suffer from my prejudices? This [question] is not taught in traditional teacher education programs. Neither [is it] required by state bureaus of teacher licensure. Indeed, it is now possible to write to any of the 50 state departments of education, stating, "I don't believe black children can ever be taught as much as white children." And still receive a teacher's license, provided one has completed the required coursework and passed a basic skills test. It seems strange that . . . we continue to select and prepare people for this sensitive occupation by examining only their grades and test scores. [26]

There is no job that requires professionals more than teaching. The most important difference between a professional and nonprofessional in any field goes far beyond being able to do the job without outside direction: It is that professionals are invested in quality.[27]

Our expectations affect the way we behave and the way we behave affects how other people respond. Teacher beliefs have a strong correlation with student achievement. Teacher behavior is goal-directed and thus is shaped by their beliefs and expectations about how to accomplish their goals. If the teacher's treatment is consistent over time, and if students do not actively resist or change it, it will likely affect their self-concepts, achievement motivation, levels of aspiration, classroom conduct, and interactions with the teacher. [28]

School community members want their interactions with others to produce desired outcomes. This attainment depends, in large measure on other's role competence.

For example, parents depend on the professional ethics and skills of school staff for their children's welfare and learning . . . a major factor in [preventing] negative parent-school relations.[29]

People who can be perceived of as models are people whose value systems are in line with what the society in general considers as imperative. Teachers are persons the students will naturally look up to and identify with because of their values and their personal qualities. [30]

Professionalism in the noblest sense denotes both heightened pride in one's work and a heightened sense of responsibility. The training of teachers was to be integral to the promise of American democracy and a perpetuation of its best principle. Education schools [hold] enormous importance in the sphere of teacher certification by their huge ideological influence in the nation's schools. [31]

Clearly then, a complete study of educational ethics and professional behavior is consistent with quality teaching—a study that must occur *prior* to the teacher's entering the classroom—not after. Delaying ethics education until a teacher begins his professional practice is putting the cart before the horse. Such a delay results in failure, frustration, and liability for both new teachers and school administrators. This trial-and-error method results in hastening the exodus of our youngest professionals from the classroom. Willingness to model ethical behavior is an effective curb against poor teaching evaluations, as well as potential legal disaster for the teacher and their school district.

Talk It Over—Ethical or Unethical?

1. A first-year middle-school band director is charging $55 per hour for individual music lessons that focus on the competitive "contest" music to be used in regional contests. Students who take the lessons are virtually guaranteed to do exceptionally well in state-level competition.
2. In 2001, a first-year teacher agreed to sponsor a local high school cheerleading squad. Midway into the first season, the teacher was arrested on campus during squad practice for embezzlement of school funds. She had, in fact, deposited several hundred dollars of fundraising money into her own personal checking account, from which she was writing checks for supplies needed by her students.

   - View the NEA code of ethics at the end of this text. Which statement did the teachers violate?
   - Did your teacher education program prepare you to know the ethical course of action in either of these cases?

HOW WILL A STATE BOARD OF EDUCATION ENFORCE AN ETHICS CODE?

States are given the legal obligation to guard the certification process of teachers and to issue all initial teacher certifications. Since colonial times, teachers have been held to a high standard of moral conduct within the community. Modern courts have underscored the "special privilege" inherent in a "unique position of trust" and authority. A teacher whose behavior "shocks the conscience" is abhorrent to the education community and the community at large. States have a vested interest in policing the ranks of teachers and in removing those who use their teaching authority to harm students or who violate ethics standards adopted by state boards of education. The state board of education issues teacher certification in compliance with legislated school code. The state can withdraw that license at any time.

The terms "licensure" and "certificate" can be vague and are used interchangeably by legislators, educators, and the general public. In the most general sense, certification is a process of legal sanction, authorizing the holder of a credential to perform specific services in the public schools of the state. Licensure, on the other hand, may be defined as the legal process by which those in professions *other than education* are authorized by the state to practice their profession before the public and to charge a fee or salary for the professional services rendered.[32] Because all states now initially certify teachers, and have complete control over the renewal of teaching certificates, clear violations of ethics standards have the potential to lead to revocation or suspension of state certificates. Official decisions are final and cannot be appealed. Although there is presently no comprehensive interstate agreement to identify teachers whose licenses have been revoked, fingerprinting and background checks are becoming commonplace across the nation. In addition, there are several private agencies that offer school districts access to their database listings of teachers convicted of misconduct. Once a state license has been revoked, a teacher may be considered unfit for any teaching position, in any state. Even in states that offer "lifetime" certificates, suspension and revocation of the certificate are possible.

States have responded to the federal call for close scrutiny of certified personnel. Ethics acts, as well as the mandated responses to code violations, vary from state to state. For example, ethics codes may be included in a school code or be promulgated by a regional or state superintendent's office, state law, a state board of education, administrative rules, and/or local school districts. Such codes are enforced via committees that have such names as Education Practice Commission, State Teacher Certification Board, Ethics Review Boards, and School Practices Commission. Legal authority is given to these entities to handle complaints and to investigate and conduct hearings regarding immoral acts, incompetence, or insubordination by teachers and school administrators. For example, the Florida State Board of Education, Education Practices Commission is empowered via state statutes (Section 231.28(1)) to investigate allegations by any individual. The Florida Department of Education Code of Ethics of the Education Profession, section 6B-1.006-2, includes the following warning: "Violation of any of these principles shall subject the individual to revocation or suspension of the individual educator's certificate, or other penalties as provided by law."[33]

The New York State Department of Education Office of School Personnel Review and Accountability is empowered by state regulations issued by the Commissioner of Education, Part 83, to investigate complaints against certificate holders (teachers, administrators, and school service workers) only: "Complaints about instances of poor moral character or illegal practice by a teacher or school administrator certified by the State of New York are investigated. Under the law, the school district superintendent must file a report with the Department upon knowledge that a certificate holder has been convicted of a crime or has committed an act that raises a reasonable question about the individual's moral character."[34]

The Illinois State Board of Education State Teacher Certification Board advises the State Superintendent of Education about certification issues such as certificate suspension and revocation, according to the state School Code, Chapter 105 5/21–23. The STCB now meets 8 to 10 times annually to hold hearings regarding suspension and revocation of certificates. "The board may request individuals to voluntarily surrender certificates, or they can continue to teach while awaiting the completion of the legal hearing process."[35]

South Dakota has authorized its Department of Education, under Senate Bill 31, to "revoke or suspend any certificate for any cause that would have prevented its issuance, including plain violation of contract, gross immorality, incompetence, violation of the code of ethics as determined by the Professional Teachers Practices and Standards Commission or the Professional Administrators Practices and Standards Commission."[36]

The New Jersey Department of Education has empowered a nine-member body that reviews, investigates, and renders decisions on complaints against school officials that allege violations of the School Ethics Act, N.J.S.A. 18A:12–21, according to the State Board of Education Code N.J.A/C. 6A:28.[37]

Finally, many states have adopted the NEA Code of Ethics verbatim, along with a review process that includes the right to withdraw teaching credentials. You will need to contact your state board of education to get a printed copy of the state standards for ethical education practice, as well as the complaint review process for allegations of contact violation, gross immorality, incompetence, or insubordination—key terms in state ethics codes.

WHAT IS THE DEFINITION OF GROSS IMMORALITY, INCOMPETENCE, AND INSUBORDINATION?

Recently, the author completed a survey of students from various teacher education programs who were in their last semester of study. In every case, the student had completed an entire course of accredited teacher preparation in one of two midwestern universities—one midsize (8,000 students) and one quite large (more than 50,000 students). Their responses to the following questions will amaze veteran teachers and school administrators:

> Do you feel confident that you can define the contractual issues of insubordination, incompetence, and immorality?
>
> More than 90 percent of 280 respondents simply said "no."
> Several responded "Maybe," "Mostly," "It's iffy," "For the most part," "Possibly—some issues are vague," or "Not in its entirety."
> One senior student responded, "I sure hope so."

In every forum with pre-service teachers or first-year teachers, the truth is revealed—a serious gap exists in preparation and in the teachers' understanding of the legal basis for ethical practice. One wonders how college graduates from highly lauded teacher education programs can miss the essential strand of professional ethical standards. Are such graduates ready to go into the public and private school classrooms? One hopeful soul speaks: "I sure hope so!"

The three "in"s that will launch a teacher "out" of professional certification include gross immorality, incompetence, and insubordination.

> *Immorality*—Actions that do not conform to principles of right conduct; actions that are willful, flagrant, or shameless and that shows a moral indifference to the opinions of the good and respectable members of the community.[38]
>
> *Incompetence*—Want of physical, intellectual, or moral ability; insufficiency; inadequacy; specific want of legal qualification or fitness. Lack of fitness to teach due to lack of knowledge of subject matter; lack of discipline; unreasonable discipline; unprofessional conduct; and willful neglect of duty.[39]
>
> *Insubordination*—Willful disregard for express or implied directions of the employer or repeated refusal to obey reasonable regulations; failure to cooperate with school administrators or to comply with contractual obligations. [40]

For example:

- Teachers who use sick leave for reasons outside the collective bargaining agreement and/or school board policy guidelines are liable for action under state ethics codes.
- Teachers who fail in their responsibility to enforce reasonable discipline in their classroom are subject to removal from the classroom through action of state ethics boards.
- Teachers who violate state standardized testing security procedures are subject to certificate revocation.
- Teachers who conduct themselves contrary to community standards for morality are at risk of removal from the classroom for gross immorality.
- Teacher actions so grossly brutal and inhumane as to be "shocking to the conscience of a reasonable person" include those that violate substantive due process rights. Punitive damages in civil court cases against the teacher will be based on this issue. Misconduct perpetrated by educators is judged by the "shocks the conscience" standard set by civil courts.

Unethical teaching behaviors may also include the following, as defined by state ethics codes and state law. Teacher conduct is unethical if the teacher has perpetrated or facilitated:

- A willful failure to report an instance of suspected child abuse.
- A failure to establish satisfactory repayment on an educational loan.
- A refusal to attend or participate in teacher meetings, training days, or professional readings.
- Conduct that violates the security, monitoring, or scoring of any assessment test.
- An intention to produce or report manipulated or artificial, rather than actual, achievement results of tests or examinations.
- Neglect or unnecessary delay in preparing statistical or other reports as required by school officers.
- A condition of health detrimental to the welfare of pupils.
- A failure to file a tax return or to pay the tax, penalty, or interest shown in a filed return.
- The abuse or neglect of a child.

State board of education hearing committees may respond to ethics violations with the following actions:

- They may decide not to renew or issue (in the case of first-year teachers) a teacher's license.
- They may pass along the case to the local school board or regional superintendent for disciplinary action, as deemed necessary.
- Recommend that the teacher be suspended for one year.
- Recommend that the teacher be suspended for up to five years.
- Recommend that the license be permanently revoked, meaning a complete loss of teaching privileges.
- Fine the teacher's school district for the unethical behavior.
- Recommend that the teacher's certificate be invalidated in other states as well (interstate "reciprocity").

Although the process is unique in each state, all states have strict time guidelines for each step in the process from complaint to hearing committee outcomes. Appeals of committee decisions are sent directly to the state superintendent, who has a vested interest in upholding the committee's decisions. Clearly, the educators' ability to continue in their chosen profession is in the balance when state ethics codes are adopted and enforced.

Case in Point

On August 13, 2003, the Illinois State Board of Education issued a news release to all media providers, detailing the unethical actions taken by one high school principal and one teacher. The pair compromised state test procedures when they allegedly opened, copied, and distributed parts of the state high school completion test, the Prairie State Exam. The media release reported to the public Illinois State Superintendent Robert E. Schiller's request that the local school board, the employer of the two educators, take appropriate disciplinary action against the two. He described his recommended action to fine the local school district for test violations. He also requested the educators to voluntarily surrender their state certificates.

Talk It Over

- Do you feel that a media release was the appropriate way to inform the public of the ongoing investigation?
- What state action would be fair to the two educators, if they refuse to surrender their teacher certification?
- If the local school board had taken no action against the teachers but the state had, what appeal process would be available to the two educators?

The key idea is that violators of state ethics codes are held to strict account within the limits of state law. Those who are found to be in violation of adopted ethics codes are in clear danger of censure of teaching credentials and loss of their teaching positions. What you do not know about your state's ethics codes will impact your career in education, whether you are a teacher or an administrator.

Finally, state boards of education are intensely involved in the quality of teacher education programs within the state. State boards of education regularly review colleges of education and make recommendations for correction when weaknesses appear in the program, as indicated by a low pass rate on state-mandated certification exams. In fact, every American college of education must report yearly demographic data and state exam pass rates and program completion rates as a part of compliance with the federal Higher Education Act, Section 207, Title II, information. In establishing the Title II reporting system, Congress focused on the public's lack of basic information about whether those who complete teacher preparation programs are prepared to teach and how state licensing and certification requirements may affect who teaches in our nation's classrooms.[41]

HOW ARE NATIONAL TEACHER EDUCATION ACCREDITATIONS IMPACTING ETHICAL AND PROFESSIONAL DISPOSITIONS?

Some radical strides toward ethics education are being taken by large associations involved in the accrediting process for colleges of education. Institutions of higher education undergo rigorous scrutiny during the accreditation process and thereafter periodically schedule review visits. Both state commissions and national associations have a hand in this critical review process. Accreditation is the official recognition accorded to an educational institution in the United States via inclusion in a list of institutions issued by an agency or organization that sets up standards or requirements. By means of accreditation, professional organizations, associations of institutions, and official state agencies make known to the public those colleges and universities, elementary and secondary school, hospitals, clinics, scientific laboratories, and other institutions serving the public that meet required standards of quality as determined by the accreditation agency.[42] The result of the accreditation journey is a top-down process of external review that ensures quality and consistency in teacher preparation programs to protect the public welfare.

One cannot refer to teacher education accrediting process in the United States without mentioning NCATE, the National Council for the Accreditation of Teacher Education, founded in 1954. The accreditation process is both prestigious and rigorous, built on actual student performance assessment by the college, rather than on standardized test scores or final course grades. That is, colleges of education that wish to continue to receive NCATE certification must reorganize teacher education courses to include many and varied opportunities for teacher candidates to thoughtfully develop, clearly demonstrate, and fairly assess student skills prior to the capstone course—student teaching. Presently, 46 states and more than 602 colleges and universities have aligned their teacher education standards with NCATE to reflect a new emphasis on professional behaviors demonstrated in the undergraduate classroom.[43] Additionally, NCATE has rallied 33 specialty professional associations (SPA), each focused on specific content or a specific professional area, to accept NCATE standards to permit a more uniform review of teacher education programs. For example, the National Middle School Association, the National Science Teachers Association, and the International Reading Association, as well as 30 other SPAs have accepted the NCATE review standards (or perhaps added a few small exceptions that can easily be accommodated) by which they will assess teacher education content preparation courses. Colleges of education covet the earned accreditation and value the process of stringent external review. Certainly this badge of excellence benefits higher education institution when they are recruiting new students for their teacher preparation programs or seeking internal funding and external grants for the program. Simply said, the stakes are quite high for universities and colleges in the teacher preparation business as they move to include the NCATE-required "dispositions" statement in the criteria they use to determine eligibility for graduation of education majors.

Pre-professional ethical understandings may be termed "dispositions." According to NCATE (standard 1), professional dispositions can be defined as "The values, commitments and professional ethics that influence behaviors toward students, families, colleagues and communities and affect students learning, motivation and development as well as the educator's own professional growth. Dispositions are guided by beliefs and attitudes related to values such as caring, fairness, honesty, responsibility and social justice."[44] The unit—the college of education—seeking NCATE initial or continuing certification must show clear and convincing proof that:

1. The unit has clearly defined the dispositions the faculty expects to observe in their students.
2. Professional dispositions are directly linked to the faculty's greater concept of professional teaching.
3. The dispositions, as demonstrated by each candidate, are consistently assessed.
4. Dispositions data are included in student records, such as a portfolio of teaching products.
5. Teacher education faculty and students know and can verbalize the dispositions that are being assessed, as well as their importance to the profession and program.
6. Dispositions are assessed at several "turning points" in the program and students are offered remedial opportunities that are designed to be fair, consistent, and open to all students.

Interestingly, the NCATE use of "dispositions" is another way of expressing a Socratic understanding of "virtues" as described earlier in this chapter.

Additionally, the Interstate New Teacher Assessment and Support Consortium (INTASC), another player in the teacher prep accreditation arena, also has expressed a desire to assess the "fitness" of new teachers by way of dispositions—that is, a teacher candidate's attitudes and values. Using the vehicle of "virtue" statements, INTASC standards supplant the teacher preparation program's own homegrown list of ethical priorities. INTASC clearly delineates statements of ethics attitudes, such as these:

> INTASC.3.H—The teacher respects students as individuals with differing personal and family backgrounds and various skills, talents and interests.
> INTASC.3.I—The teacher is sensitive to community and cultural norms.
> INTASC.3.J—The teacher makes students feel valued for their potential as people, and helps them to learn to value each other.
> INTASC.3.F—The teacher believes that all children can learn at high levels and can achieve success.[45]

Teacher education institutions have a vested interest in their continued accreditation and therefore rush to clearly verbalize program ethical expectations for students or adopt a preexisting one. Regardless of which option colleges of education take, pre-service teachers must be introduced to, reflect on, and be knowledgeable about ethical standards for professional practice.

Difficulty arises when students are assessed via ethics codes. Questions abound. Although key terms in the NCATE document on dispositions are not well defined and therefore lend themselves to highly individualistic interpretations, NCATE has led hundreds of teacher education programs into an effort to assess such dispositions, as displayed by thousands of individual teacher education candidates. How does one measure or reward motivation, intention, or attitudes apart from displayed behavior? How does one enforce and reward ethical behavior displayed by faculty members or clinical supervisors? How are glaring violations remediated if students hold notions that run contrary to the accepted norm? This conundrum forces colleges of education into a negative model for responding to most ethics codes—dealing with problematic, deficient behavior that falls short of the ethical standard being espoused. Remediation of recurring troublesome behavior brings up the potential for ultimate exclusion from the teacher education program. Unfortunately, stringent disciplinary action in turn touches upon constitutional legal protections of due process and prohibitions of discrimination. These are hurdles that will be faced in the coming years, as ethics "dispositions" statements meet the everyday practice of "walking the walk."

Case in Point

A new aspect of ethics codes has begun as a direct response to NCATE and INTASC pressure—ethics codes for student teachers. In the past, ethical behavior in college classes and programs was traditionally covered by institutional student honor codes. However, the faculties of several colleges of education have begun to crystallize their thinking regarding the ethical behavior of their student teachers by composing a higher level of honor, specifically pointed toward outstanding professional practice in clinical settings (in-school placements).

For example, the Illinois State University College of Education has described desired ethical behavior standards in "Moral Virtue" and "Intellectual Virtue" statements. Adherence to these standards is expected throughout the program, from freshman to senior year.

The Moral Virtues

1. Sensitivity toward the varieties of individual and cultural diversity.
2. Disposition and ability to collaborate ethically and effectively with others.
3. Reverence for learning and seriousness of personal and public purpose.
4. Respect for learners of all ages, with special regard for children and adolescents.

The Intellectual Virtues

1. Wide general knowledge and deep knowledge of the content to be taught.
2. Knowledge and appreciation of the diversity among learners.
3. Understanding of what affects learning and appropriate teaching strategies.
4. Interest in and ability to seek out informational and collegial resources.
5. Contagious intellectual enthusiasm and courage enough to be creative.

Talk It Over

- Could these statements be used to select student teaching placements? In what way?
- Imagine a situation in which a student could be excluded from the program on the basis of the moral virtues. How could compliance to the virtues be proven beyond a doubt?

- How would you explain the "seriousness of personal and public purpose" to a group of pre-service teachers?

- How do these statements differ from the National Education Association code of ethics requirement that "Educators shall not use professional relationships with students for private advantage"?

The appendix includes two further examples of teacher education ethics codes (dispositions) for students working to become teachers. Which would you favor for your educational institution?

The appendix of this text has several codes of ethics for teachers and for those who prepare teachers. It is perhaps the most comprehensive educational collection available. Look over the ethics codes. Locate your state's expectations for your professional behavior and the enforcement procedures. Be sure to understand the level of professional competence you will be expected to achieve to demonstrate excellent teaching in the classroom.

HOW DO SUCCESSFUL TEACHERS DISPLAY ETHICAL CARING BEHAVIOR?

Victoria Huffman, EdD, and Cindy Brubaker, EdD, RN

Noddings (*Caring: A Feminine Approach to Ethics and Moral Education*, 1984) posits that any consideration of caring naturally brings into consideration ethics, because ethics are concerned with how we treat others. According to Noddings, a relational analysis of caring is more accurately attuned to the complexity of real human relationships, such as those that exist between teachers and students. Noddings's ethic of caring has at its foundation the relation between the one-caring (teacher) and the cared-for (students). The one-caring tries to apprehend the reality of the other, which in turn arouses a feeling of "I must do something" to fulfill the other's needs. There is a commitment to act on behalf of the other. The one-caring contributes something (an attitude of caring) that is received and completed within the cared-for. The cared-for in turn gives a response back to the one-caring, which sustains the caring relation. In order for teachers to be ethically caring practitioners, they must recognize the components of ethical caring and use them to guide their pedagogical practice.

The major concepts of ethical caring that must be present in the practices of teachers are apprehending, confirmation, disposability, motivational displacement, non-rule-bound behavior, and receptivity. The final concept of ethical caring is the responsiveness exhibited by students. Apprehending is exhibited in the teacher's ability to grasp the perspectives of students. The responses from students can include a sense of satisfaction as they perceive that the teacher is working on their behalf to accomplish their goals. Confirmation is the ability of the teacher to bring about the best outcomes for students; in response, students develop trust and participate in their own learning willingly because they feel accepted, welcomed, and as if they are partners in a joint effort. Disposability is the readiness of the teacher to be available to students. A likely response is that students will approach the teacher without hesitation and will accept help. Motivational displacement is exhibited as the teacher focuses energy toward students. The students realize that the teacher is investing time and effort for their benefit. They also have a sense that the teacher is giving priority to their needs. Non-rule-bound behavior is apparent as the teacher responds to each unique situation and treats students as individuals with regard for human affections, weaknesses, and anxieties. Students have a sense that the teacher respects their cultural heritage, does not discriminate, is familiar with their special needs, and has a holistic view of their strengths and weaknesses. Teachers show that they are receptive to students by looking, listening, and feeling with them. This is more than empathy or sympathy. It involves a commitment on the part of the teacher to put aside personal needs and desires in order to concentrate on the needs of students. This commitment conveys to students that they are more important than anything else the teacher could be doing. They have a sense that their point of view is important; they initiate conversation and willingly associate with the teacher.

Noddings proposes that it is the responsibility of the teacher to create caring relationships and to facilitate the development of caring attitudes and skills within students. Herein lies a reality about ethical caring between teachers and students. The teacher must demonstrate the components of ethical caring so that students gain trust in the teacher before they become willing to respond to the teacher in a positive way that allows ethical caring relationships to develop. An ethic of caring can be taught, but it requires practice and opportunities for shared caring. Reflection, sharing, dialogue practice, and modeling are teaching modalities that can be used to teach an ethic of caring. Postsecondary educational efforts should produce more than content-prepared teachers; it should produce ethically caring practitioners who can contribute to the development of caring students.

CHAPTER 2

Drawing the Line with Students

Key Concepts

District policy
Culpability
Quid pro quo
Reasonable action
Privileged communication
Custodial parents
Official capacity
Substantive evidence
Punitive damages
Injunctive relief
Federal court
State court
Indemnification
Civil suit

This chapter will:

1. Define "official capacity" as it relates to teachers' and school administrators' performance of their duties.
2. Describe several levels of teacher and school district legal responsibilities in civil court decisions.
3. List and define several potential liability situations related to teacher-student interaction.
4. Identify several danger areas for teacher behavior.

WHAT ARE THE FOUR LEVELS OF TEACHER RESPONSIBILITY?

The four curbs to professional behavior in the classroom revolve around the following entities.

The local school board, as an arm of state government, is expected to formulate and implement policies that facilitate the effective education of the students, protect the taxpayer investment in real estate, utilize financial capital, and meet guidelines for fair employment practices set by the state. School district policy exists as it is outlined in the collective-bargaining agreement; otherwise, school board policy is a living thing, ever changing. An authoritative policy handbook is provided when a teacher is first contracted as a district employee. Too often, that material is lost or left to accumulate dust on a back shelf. The teacher then begins to make decisions based on faulty assumptions—on things remembered from school days—or follows the recommendation of other faculty who may be as clueless as the teacher is. As events occur, school board policies are revised to better meet the legal mandates of state and federal laws, as well as to ensure that local politics and priorities are reflected in the daily administration of the schools.

School policy must be followed to the letter. The school district has specific policies to follow if administrators wish to avoid legal culpability. Many school policies are written specifically to protect the district from the civil suits that most assuredly will follow on the heels of a criminal charge. School policies are crafted to protect the district and the victim, not the educator. The district will always stay on the safe legal side. That means that it will deal more stringently with the educator than with involved students or any community members. On the other hand, there is no successful legal defense for school policy that is in noncompliance with the federal constitution or state tort legislation.

Case law reveals the continuum of judicial decisions regarding school administration and teacher misconduct. These decisions are the legal precedents that drive the formulation or revision of school district policy. Civil cases that pit school districts against their employees, parents, or teacher associations have increased exponentially in the past 10 years. School boards and their administrators find themselves facing myriad state and federal civil suits in response to allegations of teacher misconduct. Case law abounds with reports of school boards that made poor decisions and/or attempted to delay or defer decisive action. In summary, teachers and school have much to lose in civil court cases that may drag on for years. An overview of applicable case law reveals the unfortunate fact that school districts and their faculties need advance training in potential legal liabilities and responsibilities. School administrators who fail to train employees regarding actions that constitute potential liability do a tremendous disservice to their employees, constituents, school boards, and, most important, students. Judicial review may come from state courts or federal courts.

Federal law is based on congressional legislative action and establishes a high bar for school district compliance in return for federal funding. Most recently, No Child Left Behind standards dictate funding options for curriculum, teacher preparation, teacher selection, teacher qualification, student proficiency testing, school administration, and school choice and mandate reporting of school accountability disclosures.[1] That legislation is simply the latest in a mountain of federal mandates placed upon our nation's schools. Just a few of the other federal mandates include the following:

Title VII of the Civil Rights Act of 1964
The Civil Rights Act of 1991.
Title IX of the Education Amendments of 1972
Title 42 under the United States Code Section 1983
U.S. Constitution, 14th Amendment—Equal Protection Clause
U.S. Constitution, 14th Amendment—Due Process Clause
U.S. Constitution, 14th Amendment—Protected Liberty
Section 504 of the Rehabilitation Act of 1973—P.L. 93–112
National Labor Relations Act
Individuals with Disabilities Education Act

State laws or state education codes vary from state to state. Some states include a statement of professional ethics that allows for termination or suspension of teacher certificates. State laws may also include antidiscrimination statutes that apply to students, school district administrators, and teachers. Fair employment practice guidelines vary considerably from state to state. Equal Employment Opportunity Commission policies are often found in state Fair Employment Practice guidelines. Remedies and timelines also differ from state to state. In addition, opinions from an attorney general's office have the impact of law.

Finally, acting as representatives of a governmental entity (a school board), school administrators and school board members may incur liability for malfeasance, misfeasance, or nonfeasance within the scope of their professional duties. The community holds schools and teachers to a high standard of conduct in their individual and official capacity. Actions by school personnel that would "shock the conscience" of reasonable persons, may result in huge punitive (punishment) damages awarded by juries.[2] In summary, school administrators are expected to exhibit clear thinking, fair practices, effective communication skills, and an in-depth knowledge of legal liabilities of teacher misconduct, along with an understanding of the repercussions for any missteps for the greater faculty and community. Not a simple task, by any means.

Together, these four areas form a comprehensive whole for the effective administration of American schools. Therefore, new faculty must be made aware of the dynamic interplay of the legal mandates that knock on the schoolhouse door.

WHY DO TEACHERS FAIL TO FOLLOW LEGAL GUIDELINES?

The professional nature of teaching demands that educators understand and nurture students. Just as teachers must encourage intellectual and emotional discovery, they also expect students to mistakes. The exact opposite is true when a teacher makes a mistake in judgment or practice. When a teacher is accused of misconduct or child abuse, more than one teacher's reputation is destroyed. Trust and confidence in the entire professional community are diminished among other teachers, students, parents, and the greater community. Parker Palmer writes: "Teachers make an easy target. For they are such a common species and powerless to strike back. We blame teachers for being unable to cure social ills that no one knows how to treat: we insist that they instantly adopt whatever solution has most recently been concocted by our national panacea machine; and in the process, we demoralize, even paralyze the very teacher who would help us find our way."[3]

New legal and ethical expectations for practicing classroom educators are not commonly covered in teacher education texts or in pre-professional field practicum. Student teachers receive little instruction in public school law and therefore often cannot describe simple legal parameters regarding liability, negligence, harassment, or professional ethics. They are, in most cases, wholly unprepared to identify problematic student behavior or to exhibit acceptable teacher behavior.

The most vulnerable teachers are our youngest professionals. Fresh- faced and idealistic, first-year teachers want to save the world. They see students as personal friends. Unsure about the boundaries of the teacher-student relationship, they often stray across professional limits of behavior. Student teachers simply do not have opportunities to practice identification of ethical teacher behaviors. Student teachers need adequate time and expert guidance to process and unlearn behaviors they may consider correct—but that in reality are clear violations of state law, federal mandates, or professional ethical standards.

Dangerous behavior patterns, learned from four years of college social interactions, and the fact that student teachers may be very close in age to their classroom students set the stage for tragedy. High school and middle school students attempt to affiliate themselves with young teachers, perceived to be young, attractive, successful, and powerful. Many student teachers are barely four years older than their classroom charges. The closeness in age encourages risky comments and behaviors by students toward their student teachers.

Another caveat related to this lack of explicit preparation is that student teachers often seek to emulate their professional mentors. Unfortunately, experienced classroom teachers often misunderstand risky behavior by students. In fact, women teachers and less experienced teachers are often targets for verbal and/or sexual abuse by students—or other faculty. Many university professors lack training in public school law or professional ethics for public school settings. Unbelievably, many problematic student teacher behaviors are accepted and/or encouraged by cooperating teachers and university professors, who misinterpret the behavior as a form of friendliness toward students.

For example, in *Doe v. Berkley County School District*, a student teacher offered to take a female high school student for a "ride in his car." Although the building principal enlightened the student teacher regarding the inappropriate offer, no record of the incident was given to the university supervisor (who rated the student as excellent in the teaching placement). One year later, now a substitute for the same district, the young man was involved in a sexual relationship with two female high school students.[4] One wonders whether, had the correct action been taken at the first sign of his poor decision making, the young man would ever have had a career in teaching. Unfortunately, not understanding that certain behaviors are inappropriate will not absolve the student (or the school district) from legal, moral, or ethical responsibility. Student teachers need the support of informed instructors to identify and assess problematic behaviors.

When a school district or teacher association attorney offers clear warnings for teachers to stay out of isolated situations or to refrain from touching students, such warnings are met with scoffing from the faculty. Teachers may be the only adults the students have on their side emotionally. In short, warnings of potential misconduct are either absent or go unheeded. All teachers must discuss and problem-solve such situations, enabling them to think ahead. Perhaps more important, colleges of education must provide teacher candidates with the skills to identify and to intervene in problematic student behavior and to avoid the appearance of wrongdoing. This chapter will equip teachers with descriptions of problematic teaching situations, summaries of pertinent law cases, and descriptions of best practices, discussed within a context of teacher advocacy.

Each teaching professional is called upon daily to face potentially critical issues that have been the impetus for court cases in the past, including student privacy, classroom discipline, and the supervision of extracurricular activities. In the next section, we present best practices for each professional challenge, discuss each in a civil-case brief, and finally, provide a short, hypothetical scenario for further discussion.

WHAT CLASSROOM DISCIPLINE GUIDELINES SHOULD BE FOLLOWED?

All teachers know that discipline sets the stage for effective learning in the classroom. In many classes, discipline takes up 80 to 100 percent of the teacher's energy for the first few weeks, while classroom rules are being taught. Although lesson planning is the perennial focus for undergraduate teacher preparation, little time is spent learning disciplinary strategies and techniques—and still less is spent on the legalities of such techniques. Many teachers still employ sarcasm and public humiliation strategies (both harmful) rather than learn new effective and positive ways to mentor and control a classroom filled with energetic, mischievous, and inquisitive kids.

Classroom discipline is an essential element in teacher competency. Teachers are expected by their school districts to maintain order in the classroom and to establish an environment conducive to learning. Not only have the courts spoken clearly on the subject of teacher control of students (in loco parentis), but the federal No Child Left Behind Act requires that any student who attends a persistently dangerous public school or who becomes a victim of a violent crime at school must be allowed to transfer to a safe public school or charter school within the district.[5] Classroom and schoolwide discipline is essential for learning to take place—the learning that results in high standardized test scores critical to the survival and funding of the school. Issues in classroom discipline include the following: detentions, blanket discipline, corporal punishment, denial of due process, child abuse (assault or battery), and child endangerment. States, as well as school districts, vary in their approaches to nonphysical discipline. Usually, courts are hesitant to micromanage classrooms and are content to allow school districts to design and implement their own policies on the use of nonphysical discipline. *Teachers must be aware of and follow all school district polices regarding nonphysical punishment of students.*

WHAT IS THE SAFEST WAY TO IMPOSE DETENTION ON STUDENTS?

Detention is the practice of keeping students in the school during recess or after school as a punishment for some offences. Although courts have upheld detention for students as a right of school districts, many liability issues are involved. Teachers are encouraged to be sure that after-class detentions are kept within legal parameters.[6] If students take a bus to and from school, often the students cannot be kept after school for any detention time. If students are kept in from recess or after lunchtime, fully certified adult supervisors must be present. Teachers cannot shift their responsibility to another teacher, staff member, or parent volunteer. Additionally, students cannot be left to their own in empty classrooms.[7] Detention poses a liability situation, unless practiced well within school district policy and legal limits.[8] The judicial concept of a "safe place" holds schools to the standard of keeping students in an environment free of potential harm.[9]

Case in Point

Graham v. Charleston City School Board, 204 S.E.2nd 384, S.C. (1974)

A second-grade girl was held for detention after school. No parental notification was given so that the child could be taken home from school by her parents. Her walk home was along the edge of a busy highway. The child was hit and killed by a truck.

Talk It Over

A high school coach kept three boys after school to practice throwing pitches in preparation for an upcoming softball game. The coach was called away and left the boys on the softball field. The coach alerted a custodian who was mowing the field that the students were on the field and asked him to observe the practice. Shortly thereafter, the boys began to throw pitches at each other. In the melee, one sustained an eye and facial injury. Where does the responsibility rest? With the coach? With the staff member? With the students, who were mature enough to understand the concept of endangerment and reckless behavior? With the school administrator who hired the coach? Should the school board be held liable for ineffective policies regarding supervision of high school athletes?

Best-Practice Overview

Do not hold students after school for any reason. If you must, be sure to provide *written notice to parents 24 hours beforehand* that includes information as to when the child will be serving detention and why the child is being held at school. Include at least three school phone numbers for an emergency contact situation, and release the child only into the hands of a custodial parent at the end of the detention. Always offer an alternative punishment for those parents who must have childcare for children after school and who cannot provide individual transportation for the child. If the detention is to be served during school hours, be sure the child is not left in an isolated situation at any time. If necessary, place the child in a school library, front office, or counselors' office with certified supervision at all times.

WHAT IS BLANKET DISCIPLINE?

Blanket discipline is the practice of imposing a disciplinary measure on an entire class or group of students for the infractions of a few or a single student—for example, all students present in a hallway are punished due to vandalism that occurred while they were in that area. The courts agree that punishments must be meted out on an individual basis—not by means of a broader classification (such as being in the vicinity of an infraction).[10]

Case in Point

Rolando v. School Directors, 358 N.E.2nd 945, Ill (1976)

A sixth-grade teacher who failed to get good control over his classroom was admonished by school administrators to gain control the best way he knew how. The teacher purchased a two-foot electric cattle prod.

The teacher then administered the prod shock to any student who did not respond to his direction. The school board fired the teacher; the judge reinstated him with back pay.

Talk It Over

Students attending a high school pep rally acted in an inappropriate manner by throwing condoms at the cheerleading squad and their sponsor. School administrators punished all the students who were seated in a general area of the bleachers by refusing to admit the students to an afterschool basketball game.

Best-Practice Overview

You must be able to identify the exact student who has committed the infraction for appropriate disciplinary action. You may not apply punishments, academic or nonacademic, to any entire group or to all representatives of one gender or race. If you are not sure of the identity of an exact perpetrator, simply said—do not assign a punishment. Wait until you can identify a specific student and provide clear evidence that a certain student is at fault.

WHAT IS CHILD ENDANGERMENT?

Child endangerment occurs when a child is placed in an environment in which harm is very likely to occur. If students are placed in or near an area such as an outside hallway, a playground wall, or an empty classroom to "cool off" during time away from a disruptive situation, full supervision must be available at all times for that child. The use of time-out areas or hallways for sitting out an activity without the provision of fully certified supervision is a clear form of child endangerment, and the teacher will be considered liable for any injury to the child.[11] Teachers and the school district will be held accountable for students who were able leave the school ground without permission due to negligence in supervision.[12]

Case in Point

Vaugh v. Orleans Parish School Board, 802 So.2nd 967 (La. Ct. App. 2001)

A second-grade student was threatened and then sexually assaulted in a secluded classroom area while the teacher graded papers at her desk. The school board was taken to task by parents who said the teacher failed to supervise the class. The teacher declined responsibility because the students were supposed to be working independently at the time of the assault.

Talk It Over

An art teacher allows students to toss pencils across the room during work time. One student is struck and sustains a serious eye injury from the sharpened pencils. What part did the teacher's action of allowing student to throwing pencils play in the liability of the school board?

Best-Practice Overview

Never place a child out of your direct sight lines as a punishment. Plan an area within the confines of the classroom that can serve as a place to help a child quiet down, or allow a certified person to walk the child to the front office for further interventions. Even when the student is left inside the classroom, a teacher must effectively supervise the student. No student should be ignored or isolated due to poor supervision by the certified instructor.[13]

WHAT IS STUDENT DUE PROCESS?

Federal constitutional rights under the Fourteenth Amendment include the opportunity for any citizen to hear any charges against him and the opportunity to answer the charges before a fair tribunal.[14] The courts have clearly stated that due process is not meant to slow or delay effective punishment needed to ensure an orderly environment in schools. If the infraction could result in suspension or expulsion, effective due process for all students is required.[15]

Case in Point

Goss v. Lopez, 419 U.S. 565 (1975)

Students involved in a general disturbance were suspended by school principals for up to 10 days without a hearing where the exact charges against them could be heard. Many of the students denied any wrongdoing. The court found that students have a right of property in their education as well as in their good name and reputation and must be granted full due-process hearings. Suspensions are permitted without prior hearing if the student poses a threat to persons, property, or the academic program; however, hearings for each student as an individual must be granted in a reasonable amount of time after the student is removed from the school setting.

Talk It Over

Students who attended a local football game vandalized a school bus used to transport the opposing team, throwing canine feces, dead chickens, and garbage into the interior of the bus. The damage delayed the visiting team's return to its home school by several hours. The cost to clean the interior of the bus was considerable. The middle school principal expelled the group of 20 eighth graders for the entire semester before the school day began the following morning. What due process must be given for the expulsion to be legal and binding for the students?

MAY TEACHERS USE CORPORAL PUNISHMENT?

Corporal punishment has been defined as "the infliction of bodily pain as a penalty for disapproved behavior."[16] Several states have refused school personnel the right to swat students for disciplinary infractions. On the other hand, several states do allow limited corporal punishment administered under specific standards; for example, it must not be inflicted in anger or frustration, and it can be administered only with paddles approved by the school board.

When good judgment and professional preparation are displaced by emotion, tragedies happen. Since the case of *Garcia by Garcia v. Miera*, an episode of horror in which an elementary school student was beaten by two adults (a teacher and a school administrator) with a broken wooden paddle, leaving the child with a two-inch cut, many civil court cases have mandated the use of a "shocks the conscience" standard. The "shocks the conscience" standard is applied to teacher actions so grossly excessive as to be shocking to the conscience of a reasonable person. Such actions always violate substantive due-process rights. Punitive damages against the teacher will be based on this issue: Did the teacher's actions amount to a "brutal and inhumane abuse of official power, literally shocking the conscience" of reasonable persons? For example, consider the following:

- A mentally disabled student who was locked in a bathroom for several hours and ordered to clean a school lavatory of feces.[17]
- A five-year-old student who was tied and duct-taped to a principal's desk for two hours.[18]

One wonders how a professional community can still commit such glaring errors in judgment in choosing the appropriate response to student behavior. A lack of knowledge regarding the policy and practice of professional education is replaced with raw anger or frustration.

Case in Point

Ingraham v. Wright, 430 U.S. 651 (1977)

A student who was slow to respond to a teacher's instructions was given more than 20 whacks with a large paddle while he was being held over a table in the principal's office. A second student, also paddled, placed a hand behind his back to stop the force of the paddling, sustaining an injury to his arm. Both students were injured in the paddling. What is the difference between school corporal punishment and child abuse?

Talk It Over

A student who was disrupting classroom instruction was grabbed by the collar and forcibly taken to the hallway by the instructor. The student hit his arm on the classroom window and broke the safety glass, sustaining a serious injury. What responsibility did the teacher have for the doorway injury to the student? What responsibility did the student have for his own injury?

Best-Practice Overview

Do not use corporal punishment for any reason; find another way to deal with the infraction. Remember, when disciplining students enrolled in special education settings or those students identified as 504 students, the student's IEP must guide any discipline. The first question the teacher will need to ask is "Did the problem behavior arise out of the student's disability?" Special accommodation must be made when that honest answer is "yes."

Be sure to follow all school district discipline guidelines, and keep clear documentation of all punishments meted out to students.

The ramifications of using corporal punishment range widely. Cruel and unusual punishment, mentioned in the Eighth Amendment to the U.S. Constitution, can be applied only to criminals, not to students in school settings.[19] Teachers are subject to liability and endangerment charges in civil court, as well as to child abuse and assault/ battery charges in criminal court. Teachers should not impose the common sports penalties of 100 pushups or squat thrusts.[20] Neither can they use public humiliation techniques such as requiring students to stand touching their toes for 10 to 12 minutes.[21] Locker-room jokes and funny punishments quickly lose their humor in the eyes of a civil court judge.

WHAT LIABILITIES DO EXTRACURRICULAR ACTIVITIES POSE FOR THE TEACHER?

The willingness to sponsor afterschool activities offers an open employment door for new teaching professionals. That is, many teachers are hired not solely for their professional accreditation and experience but also for their willingness to act as sponsors for extracurricular activities. Such activities place a strain on new teachers because of three factors:

1. Many activities occur outside school hours.
2. School board policies that govern such activities may not exist or may not be clearly communicated to those who need the information, such as sponsors.
3. Fundraising is often an integral part of the financial lifeline for the activity.

Let's look at each of these factors.

First, afterschool hours pose a threat to both students and teachers in various ways. From football games to speech contests, teachers spend hours after school and on weekends doing their jobs. It is no wonder the largest group of teachers accused of misconduct are extracurricular and electives teachers. Music directors, cheerleading sponsors, drama directors, and athletic coaches are most at risk for allegations of negligence or endangerment. Activity sponsors have difficulty finding credible adult witnesses to an event that allegedly happened after play practice at 9:00 P.M. in the school auditorium. The student whose parents are consistently late to pick her up after a school activity is tempted to stay to help the teacher with daily tasks. The isolated situation is a danger for teacher and student. Additionally, field trips are an especially dangerous time for sponsors. Students act differently away from the formal confines of school. The informal environment engenders informal relationships and lackadaisical attitudes toward school policy guidelines.

Second, policies that enable the school board to govern afterschool activities may be absent. Worse yet, they may exist, but only in a dusty handbook. Sponsors who have little teaching experience will model their teaching practice on the way they remember that activity being done in their home district. Teacher mistakes—now repeated by a second generation—are taken into a new context and within a new set of professional parameters. New teachers, overwhelmed at the start of school, may be simply surviving until the dismissal bell. These same teachers often are given little or no notice of policy guidelines that would ensure their success and support by the school board, should the worst happen.

Last, fundraising is an area of great danger for many new teachers and sponsors. Embezzlement charges can be leveled against a teacher in the event that she simply pays for any supplies herself and then takes repayment when the money is available from profits or school funds. Nothing must go into or out of a teacher's personal account. Many schools employ a treasurer who will insist on completed documentation before funds are made available for an afterschool activity. Although this may slow the funding, it is safer for the sponsor as well as the school administration. Unfortunately, often the new sponsor knows very little about procedures designed by the school board to pass an annual review by external auditors. Please remember, embezzlement is a criminal charge, and misuse of school funds is considered incompetence—a reason for discharge. The factors are quite volatile for the new sponsor.

Case in Point

Kelso v. Southfield Public Schools Board of Education, 2005 Mich. App. Lexis 2618

A teacher serving as athletic director staffed a concession stand with his relatives. Money began to be missing from both ticket sales and concession sales. In spite of a clear administrative directive, the athletic director failed to turn over the funds directly after the school event was finished and to follow guidelines for selling tickets to the activity.

Talk It Over

A middle school cheerleading sponsor was arrested for embezzlement of approximately $1,000. The case involved fundraising profits used by the sponsor to purchase pep rally supplies, socks and hair bows for the squad, and pictures of the individual members and to pay entry fees for competition events. The sponsor placed all fundraising profits from cookies sales into her personal account and used the money as needed. If a complete and accurate record of how the funds were spent was produced, why arrest the teacher?

Best-Practice Overview

All sponsors must begin their sponsorship with a quick trip to the building principal with a list of 22 questions in hand. The questions should include the following:

1. How is money handled for the activity?
2. Is there any faculty member who was the former sponsor (to get an idea of how the activity was last administered)?
3. What is the district policy on how and when practices may be scheduled?
4. May I include a parent volunteer to aid in the sponsorship?
5. How will transportation be arranged throughout the district?
6. Is there a requirement that students with failing grades or inappropriate behavior be excluded from the activity? Can students be cut?
7. What permission slips must be signed by parents?
8. Is there an honor code for students to follow?
9. What is the school board position on including boys and girls in the activity?
10. Are there separate facilities for each group?
11. What is the timeline for starting practice out of season?
12. What medical resources and rules will the district expect teachers to follow in case of student injury?
13. What governing body handles the rule for interscholastic competition?
14. Am I allowed to fundraise? Under what condition?
15. Are out-of-state or overnight trips allowed under school board policy?
16. How are school facilities reserved for the practice times?
17. Are there school board polices that govern the release of pictures taken during practice or performance?
18. What is the board policy regarding uniforms or dress codes?
19. What is the board policy regarding the release of students to parents after games or performances?
20. May I plan group award dinners for the end of the season? What are the approved locations?
21. What safety equipment is required for students?
22. What are the emergency phone numbers for school administration members should it be necessary to call someone?

Should the teacher fail to get the school administrator's direction regarding each element of team sponsorship, serious communication problems will result in poor coaching, student/parent dissatisfaction, possible legal action, and a dismal end to the season. Finally, if the teacher is assigned extracurricular duty, such as attendance at a football game, that teacher must comply. The results of nonattendance for the teacher include two "career-ending" situations. First, the school district will view the refusal to attend as insubordination. Second, the teacher is liable for any unforeseen events that happen in his assigned area, such as a student injury or student fight.[22] Although the school district has the right to assign additional duties according to school district needs, the teacher must be compensated for the additional time spent outside the school day as per the collective-bargaining agreement.

MAY TEACHERS TRANSPORT STUDENTS?

At no time should teachers transport students in a private vehicle. Students who are transported by teachers are at risk for injury from car accidents, lack of appropriate restraint, and poor supervision.[23] Additionally, given the fact that at some point the teacher and the student will be the only occupants of the vehicle, there is a risk that allegations of sexual misconduct will arise.[24] Placing a student in the teacher's private vehicle also provides an opportunity for the student to charge the teacher with misconduct. Court cases have described incidents in which the car a teacher was driving was involved in an accident and students have been maimed or killed. Some teachers have taken students to unsafe houses. Teachers have used private cars to transport entire teams. Once a student was hit and killed while exiting the car onto a busy highway. School administrators and quasi-administrators, such as counselors, are indemnified (covered by insurance in the performance of their official duties) by their school board. Teachers are not.

Case in Point

Gorton v. Doty, 69 P2nd 136, Ida. (1937)

A teacher who was driving members of a football team to a game was involved in a car crash, and some of the students were injured. The court held the students were not "guests" in the car; rather, the teacher was acting for the school district as its agent in the transportation. The teacher's auto insurance refused to cover any medical costs. The school district said that approved transportation was available from the district but was not requested by the teacher. The court held the teacher personally liable for all costs. Private automobile insurance does not cover the transportation of students in a teacher's privately owned vehicle.

Talk It Over

A teacher helping to return students to their home school after a school basketball game allows two students to go home together. The teacher allows both students to exit the car knowing that one is not returning home but rather plans to stay at the other student's home. The one student is raped by the other. Who is to blame?

Best-Practice Overview

Do not place yourself in an automobile alone with students. You should not transport students in your own vehicle, because of the liability risk. Furthermore, you should not get in a student's car for a quick run to the local store. Any time you are in an isolated situation, you have spawned a "he said-she said" situation. Should you stop to get gasoline and perhaps purchase snacks for the student, there will be eyewitnesses who can testify that you were purchasing treats for a child. If you follow that action with any prolonged isolation or if there is a time gap in your travel, you have a situation tailor-made for an allegation of sexual misconduct. The only recourse a teacher has, when pressed to take a student home, is to notify a school administrator. Be sure to have all emergency numbers. The school administrator may come to get the child. Failing that, the teacher must notify the local police. The officers will take the student home and ensure the house is the correct residence and that a responsible adult is present.

MAY TEACHERS LEND MONEY TO STUDENTS?

Although the courts have not spoken on the practice of teachers lending money to students, there is no reason to do such an act—even if solicited by the parent via a note to the teacher. The fact that a teacher has given the money is enough to show a quid-pro-quo relation. The term "quid pro quo" usually refers to an improper use of power in a "something given or something withheld in exchange" relationship. Money fits the definition of something given for certain favors expected by or for the teacher. Such favors could include sexual satisfaction. The *St. Louis Post-Dispatch*, on March 8, 2001, ran a headline that graphically depicts the sensationalism possible when students explain the loan to the media—"Money to Disrobe!"

Teachers are hired as representatives of the school board. As such, teachers must disdain any show of favoritism toward particular students. When approached for money, teachers should refer students to the school counselor or administrator, who can provide the family with information regarding community agencies that can help. Teachers should not offer financial support or loans to any student or parent in the school district—or those potentially affected by the teacher's performance.

Talk It Over

A second-grade teacher is given a handwritten note from a parent asking for a loan of $50, to be repaid at the end of the month in food stamps. The teacher knows that this child is at risk of physical punishment by the parent and fears that a negative response will place the student in danger. The teacher agrees to give the parent the money and says that no repayment is necessary.

Best-Practice Overview

Teachers must never send money to parents of students. Eschew all business deals with parents of students in your direct charge. Protect all teachers' wallets and purses behind locked doors. Funds frequently turn up missing from school desks, lockers, or cash boxes kept inside the school building—regardless of the socioeconomic level of the surrounding neighborhood. If teachers purchase fundraising products from students (i.e., Girl Scout candy or cookies), be sure to note the exact reason on any personal check, and do not give the student cash for any reason. Also, do not expect to see the materials you purchased. No school administrator will enforce the delivery of food or gifts purchased by teachers. Buyers beware! In the event of a lunch money request, go directly to the cafeteria and offer any money to the lunch personnel; do not give the student cash. Finally, expect all money *not* to be repaid or returned, even in the event the funds were stolen from the teacher's desk or private vehicle. No school district policy will ever ensure that stolen money is returned by the culprit.

MAY TEACHERS GIVE MEDICAL AIDE TO STUDENTS?

In the 1960s, the top drawer in the teacher's desk held essential medical supplies—bandages, aspirin, and a nickel for a sanitary napkin. That was the norm; now, teacher medical supplies must be limited to a hall pass—to get the student to the front office or school nurse, if available. Medical care must be left to those most qualified (as well as insured) to administer it. Front-office secretaries are indemnified by the school district in case a student must take medicines on a regular basis. Unbelievably, school secretaries are called upon to do blood testing and to give injections to students—with little or no training.[25] The potential for mistakes and misinformation is staggering. As more students are placed on medications distributed during the school day, school districts will be forced to find more effective and efficient ways to hold up their responsibility as part of the continuum of care begun in a physician's office.

Teachers are held to a court standard of "reasonable action," defined as the actions a reasonable person in the occupation would do in light of the circumstance. Most teachers do not have medical degrees. Therefore, teachers must not give a slight " pass-over" medical intervention in case of accident or student complaint and then require the student to continue in classroom activities. The courts have spoken in several civil cases related to student deaths due to poor teacher intervention or lack of intervention. For example, a Nebraska football player with a closed head injury was encouraged to continue play; a Kansas student died from heat exhaustion following a practice.[26] Consider the example of a first-grade student pushed down during recess. His broken collarbone was treated by his teacher with a wet paper towel.[27] Failing to treat classroom injuries constitutes willful or wanton neglect. School personnel must refer the student for treatment by a competent person. Teachers simply cannot diagnose injury or the treatment unless they are certified physicians.

Mandated reporters are persons who, if in the performance of their occupational duties they have reasonable cause to suspect that a child has suffered harm as a result of child abuse or neglect, are required by law to immediately report the incident to child protection agencies. As mandated reporters of suspected child abuse or neglect, teachers simply do not have a legal option for refusing or ignoring physical signs of abuse. Neither can they ignore a direct disclosure of abuse by the student or a credible witness. In 1974, Congress passed the Child Abuse Prevention and Treatment Act (PL93–147). Since that time, all states have implemented state statutes requiring the immediate reporting of child abuse.

All teachers must have a listing of the characteristics and symptoms of child abuse or neglect and must know them well. One student disclosed sexual abuse by an uncle to her social studies teacher. The teacher did nothing and was held accountable by the trial court.[28] In the event a student threatens suicide, teachers must get a counselor to help that child immediately. The teacher must then also notify the parent that such a threat was made. The teacher's professional responsibility as a representative of the school district is to refer students who need specialized services to those most qualified to help—perhaps a physician or a counselor. Teachers should not refer parents to a specific provider but should make a general recommendation for a type of care (i.e., eye examination) by a competent professional. In short, a certified teacher does not meet the legal qualifications for a certified counselor or physician.

Case in Point

Guerrieri v. Tyson, 24 A.2nd 468, Pa. (1942)

A 10-year-old boy had an infection on the little finger of his right hand. The child asked not to participate in a volleyball game held during physical education class. Two teachers kept the boy after school in an attempt to give him medical attention. The boy's hand was submersed in a heated pan of water for 10 minutes. The boy's hand was badly burned and permanently disfigured.

Talk It Over

A teacher intercepted a note from one student to another describing a suicide pact between the two. The teacher spoke privately to both students in a short hallway conference. Both students assured the teacher that the note had been a hoax to get attention from another student. The teacher destroyed the note and ended her involvement. In three weeks, five students attempted suicide in a pact to end their lives in the same hour. Three completed the suicide attempt; two failed and received treatment in a professional facility. Was the teacher at fault? Were the parents at fault? Were the surviving students at fault?

Best-Practice Overview

Whenever a student complains about an injury or illness, allow the student to go to the person designated by the school district as a first responder. Do not wait for visual signs of an injury or illness. Teachers cannot see headaches, stomach problems, intestinal distress, or muscle aches. Teachers cannot make cavalier medical decisions based on a "stiff-upper-lip" philosophy. If the student consistently complains about illness during class, contact the parents about the loss of class time, document the situation, and notify a direct supervisor. Do not attempt to dissuade the student or to delay treatment. Watch all classroom activities for safety issues, and be sure to lock classroom doors when the classroom is empty. Students who enter empty shop classes or home economics or art rooms may be hurt on the equipment in the unsupervised area.

Students who disclose they are or have been victims of child abuse must be taken to a counselor or school nurse immediately. The teacher must follow up with a call to child protection services, for which there is a tollfree number in every phone directory. Students in emotional distress or who write notes focused on death or hurting themselves must be taken to a school nurse, administrator, or school counselor immediately. Teachers must notify the parent of such a situation immediately. Teachers may not abdicate their responsibility in any way. The courts will hold teachers responsible for taking effective action within the parameters of their certification status. The right to a "privileged communication" will not be granted to a teacher who holds a student's comments in trust. A teacher who has had a student commit suicide will always ask herself, "What if I had known?" For teachers who scoff at such advice—remember that your reputation, career, and integrity are most at stake in court, not to mention the safety and wellbeing of the students entrusted to your professional care.

WHAT MUST TEACHERS KNOW ABOUT STUDENT PRIVACY LAWS?

Mentioned in Article IV of the U.S. Constitution, security in private papers is a keystone of American law. The bedrock federal mandate for protecting the student's right to privacy in school records is the Family Education Rights and Privacy Act, or FERPA (20 U.S.C. subsection 1232g:34 CFR Part 99). The act applies to all schools that receive funds from the federal government. The act also outlines a right of redress for federal complaints against any educational provider who violates the student's protected rights under FERPA. Students and their parents have been granted the right to access all educational records. Parents may also demand a fair, impartial hearing and the removal from the record of any troublesome comments. Privacy issues and liabilities center around four items. They include the following:

1. *Publicity given to private life,* such as a negative fact put into a school newspaper. An example would be a reference to a student who has been arrested for shoplifting.
2. *Publicity that places a person in false light,* such as placing inaccurate information in a student file that casts that student in a negative light for future educators. An example is a teacher notation that reads, "Do not turn your back on this student—he steals."
3. *Appropriation of name or likeness,* such as the unauthorized use of student pictures or names in any medium disseminated beyond the school walls. An example is a high school yearbook picture of a wheelchair-bound student with the caption "the winner of the 40-yard dash."
4. *Intrusion upon seclusion,* for example recording personal information in permanent files for future use. An example is a teacher notation that reads, "Child smelled of feces before being made to wash."

Additionally, there is potential for suits for defamation of character if a teacher's critical notations in student records are brought into the courts. For example, a notation that a student was a "manic wacko" would be damaging to the student's reputation and might be grounds for a suit.

Finally, student privacy includes the search and seizure of students' materials in or out of school lockers, as has been detailed by the courts for the past 30 years. The case law is too massive to deal with all aspects of protected materials, protected searches, and lawful action by school administrators or law enforcement personnel. This is a very sensitive and active subject for civil court action. The case law continues to unfold as athletes are tested for drugs, schools search for weapons, and teachers seek to identify potentially violent students post–Columbine High School.

Case in Point

Merriken v. Cressman, 364 F. Supp. 913 (1973)

A Pennsylvania school district attempted to implement an early-intervention program for students who may have used drugs. Targeted students were identified by their schoolmates and teachers. Potential students for the program were invited to participate by letters to their parents. Participation in the program would have been noted in their permanent education records. Parents sought to have the identification criteria enjoined (stopped) by a local court on the basis of invasion of privacy and stigmatization of the students. The court agreed.

Talk It Over

The middle school yearbook has a long history of placing teasing or humorous titles under the pictures of each eighth grader. The staff this year plans to give each student an alias name drawn from current musical groups, such as Bare Naked Ladies or Beastie Boys. Teacher sponsors, who are local university students, have given their approval.

Best-Practice Overview

All written records, including anecdotal records, must meet certain criteria outlined in the Buckley Amendment to the Family Education Rights and Privacy Act of 1974. This standard requires that all records, including "teacher or counselor ratings and observations," be open for parent inspection and review. For the classroom teacher, this means only private professional notes may be kept from the legal guardian. Such notes are considered personal instructional notes and are the sole property of the teacher.[29] If teachers share notes, such as to support a disciplinary referral to advisory personnel or to inform school administration, the notes must be open for inspection by the parent or legal representative. The rule, simply stated, is this—if the notes are shared for any reason, they become an official record. Teachers must be certain of what they write, include only observable behaviors, and keep the notation neutral in tone.

The practice of grading assignment papers in class, then calling out the grades for the teacher to record is a common one. The U.S. Supreme Court has approved having the class involved in the grading but not the public disclosure of the individual student grade.[30] Teachers should be aware of students' potential emotional response to lackluster grades and should be proactive. If teachers must utilize student grading, they may find that taking up the papers to record the grades at a later time is the safest procedure. Certainly students should never be allowed to record grades in a grade book or online program or to grade a test or assignment that has great impact on promotion decisions.

Finally, do not search any student or bookbag. Teachers may detain and observe students until school administrators or security personnel arrive on the scene. But, teachers should never be involved in any search of students or their materials at any time.

WHAT CONSTITUTES SEXUAL HARASSMENT OR ABUSE BY STUDENTS OR FACULTY?

Sexual harassment by both school employers and students is a common occurrence in the modern American school. Few if any studies have investigated the question of sexual harassment toward school faculty. In one study conducted by the American Association of University Women, 36 percent of high school students reported that students do indeed sexually harass teachers and other school personnel. The AAUW's research concluded what nearly every survey and study shows—that sexual harassment is directed more at women than men.[31] Informal conversations with classroom educators continue to affirm that girls and boys in secondary settings also harass male teachers. Teachers most at risk for harassment seem to be the young professional women faculty[32] and teachers of extended-day subjects such as athletics, music, art, and drama.[33]

What do elementary, middle, and high school students know about sexual harassment? Although 81 percent of students surveyed reported they had been the recipient of sexual harassment at school, more than half of the students (54 percent) reported that they had been *both harasser and harassed.*[34] Furthermore, the number of girls and boys who have sexually harassed others is about equal (52.9 percent of boys to 52.5 percent of girls).[35] Clearly, the degree of sexual knowledge and the incidence of overt sexual behavior by students have increased in the past 10 years. Although practicing classroom teachers will wholeheartedly agree, many are completely unprepared to become targets for inappropriate student behavior and sexually oriented comments.

Kids will be kids. Unfortunately, kids may also mimic the worst adult behavior. Sadly, many students and teachers are unable to identify peer-to-peer sexual harassment behaviors. According to the Office of Civil Rights, a behavioral definition of sexual harassment would include:

1. Flipping up skirts
2. Shouting obscenities
3. Leaving obscene messages
4. Displaying pictures with sexual content
5. Sending notes or letters of a sexual nature
6. Spreading rumors about a person's sexual orientation
7. Promulgating humor or jokes about sex
8. Inserting sexual innuendoes in comments
9. Making phone calls of a sexual nature
10. Pulling down shorts.[36]

Such behaviors are common occurrences in many middle and secondary school hallways and lunchrooms. Kids enjoy pushing the limits of acceptable behavior. From student art to school yearbooks, attempts to control sexual content constitute an ongoing battleground for elementary and secondary teachers.

Why do students act out sexually harassing behaviors? Students themselves provide the following reasons:

1. "It's just part of school; it's no big deal" (39 percent)
2. They think the person likes it (28 percent)
3. They want a date with the person (24 percent)
4. Their friends encouraged them to do it (24 percent)

Teachers must be aware that sexual harassment can be student-to-student, student to teacher, or teacher to teacher or can involve school staff as well as administrators. Former Supreme Court Justice Sandra Day O'Connor wrote, "Sexual harassment ... is an all too common aspect of the educational experience."[37] In fact, students do exhibit sexually harassing behavior toward school faculty and peers. The U.S. Department of Justice tracks sexual assault, rape, and sexually oriented verbal assault reports from selected school districts across the nation. Amazingly, in one year (1996–1997), approximately 2,500 rapes, sexual assaults, or other student-to-student sexual batteries were reported. More than 400 incidents were at the elementary school level. From 1995 to 1999, more than 73,000 incidents of violence (which includes sexual battery and rape) *against teachers* were reported.[38] Furthermore, many incidents go unreported.

Important federal mandates that define sexual harassment and avoidance training, as well as procedural due process, have been outlined in two major laws.

Title VII of the Civil Rights Act of 1964 permits victims of employment discrimination based upon race, color, national origin, religion, or sex to collect compensatory damages for sexual harassment (a form of sexual discrimination). It is enforced by the Equal Employment Opportunity Commission. Several policy guidance papers are available for school administrators from the Equal Employment Opportunity Commission. Remedies may include injunctive relief and compensatory and punitive damages, within limitations.

Title IX of the Education Amendments of 1972 covers all institutions that receive federal aid. This federal statute is enforced by the Office of Civil Rights and protects victims of sex discrimination. The revised 2001 Office of Civil Rights policy guidance on sexual harassment situation provides standards for determining an institution's liability. The Office of Civil Rights provides guidelines for filing a grievance, filing a complaint, and conducting an investigation and includes information on program definitions and limitations, time limits for filing, confidentiality issues, and compliance reviews of school district. Remedies include monetary damages for suffering and emotional distress, future medical or therapeutic costs, attorney's fees, or lost wages or other job-related losses; reinstatement or promotion; tuition refunds; and injunctive relief requiring schools to change policy or training policy. It is important to note that even if a plaintiff loses in a court decision, she may file a complaint with the Office of Civil Rights. All districts must designate a Title officer, a school district administrator trained in Title IX compliance. In most cases, that school officer is the school district superintendent or associate superintendent.

Teachers and school administrators must begin to look at teacher behavior through the lens of federal guidelines, school policy, and professional ethical constraints. As a general rule, each of the following suggestions will serve the teacher in a most beneficial manner. Curbing professional practice to include them is a benefit to all stakeholders in the classroom. Teachers will be safer and more productive in their career. Students will be safer and more productive in their learning. Parents, as well as school administrators, will be rewarded in the confidence and trust they have placed in the school faculty.

Teachers must be aware of student behavior and intervene as soon as any suggestive behavior is observed in any school setting. Further, school districts must identity a Title IX officer to whom complaints can be addressed. School policy must include a process for filing and hearing complaints regarding sexual harassment against teacher, staff, or students. At no time can teachers allow behavior that condones or models sexually tainted comments or jokes. Clearly, this is a high-priority issue that will become more controversial in the near future. As a result of increasing teacher retirements, the American teaching population will become younger and lack a pool of experience from which to draw.

Case in Point

Randi W. v. Muroc Joint Unified School Dist., 60 Cal. Rptr. 2nd 263, 929 P.2nd 582 (1997)

Favorable job references were given to a teacher who had a history of sexual improprieties with his students. The district hired him on the basis of the positive reference comments made by the former district. The parent of a 13-year-old student who was sexually assaulted by the teacher—now an assistant principal—filed suit and named both school districts as negligent. The court found for the parent on both negligence and fraud claims.

Talk It Over

The walls of the boys' bathroom in a high school is scribbled with names of girls and slurs to their personal reputation. By law, the school is expected to remove those comments. The school custodian does remove the graffiti once but fails to correct a reapplication of the writing. The parents of one of the girls files suit on sexual harassment claims. Who is at fault?

BEST-PRACTICE OVERVIEW—DRAWING THE LINE WITH STUDENTS

Is it possible to identify *potentially* dangerous situations? Can teachers be proactive? What situations must teachers or anyone dealing with young people seek to avoid? General rules for high quality teaching include the following:

1. *Do not tease with flirtatious overtones.* Kids like it when you tease with them. They understand that you are kidding in good-natured fun. Not true. Ask yourself whether, if taken out of context, your words could stand on their own merit. You can be certain your comments will be taken out of context. Title IX guidelines

regarding sexual harassment clearly delineate limits to humor. The same comment you think is quite funny may send a completely different message to the listener. Any potential juror will be instructed to consider the perception of the victim rather than the intent of the perpetrator. Simply said, don't joke in a sexual or flirtatious manner with students or faculty members. Students just may take you seriously, and faculty members will remember that off-the-cuff comment. Be careful what you say in the classroom or faculty lounge and during extracurricular activities. Your words may return cast in a very different light.

2. *Never be alone in the classroom with a student.* When you direct a student to return to the classroom to finish an assignment, you must include several students in the grouping or arrange for a neutral location. Classrooms have restricted sight lines; just leaving the door to the hallway open will not serve the purpose of ensuring a credible witness for the teacher. Teachers must set up a situation where there is another responsible party to neutralize any rumor. If that is impossible or poses great inconvenience, perhaps the student could finish the assignment in a counseling room, a library, the principal's office, or another classroom where class is continuing.

3. *Stay out of isolated situations after school—for your own safety.* Don't stay in the classroom alone after school dismissal. Should a student return, it will be difficult to keep the atmosphere above suspicion. Close and lock the door to your classroom. Place a sign that reads, "I'll be right back." Students in a hurry will not stay. Other students may wait for a few minutes and then leave you a note in return. Simply said, do not allow entry by a single student; just don't answer the door. You might also work after school in the teacher's lounge, library, or computer room, where visibility is not an issue.

4. *Avoid expressions of physical affection.* Several teacher associations have provided a list of appropriate physical gestures. Past "approved" contacts have included touching the upper arm, patting the back, shaking hands, or putting an arm around the shoulder. Because this constraint seems too surgical for teachers, they simply ignore the advice. In fact, current court cases prove that there simply is no "approved" physical contact appropriate in all settings between student and teacher. The best advice—touch students only in a neutral manner and in the presence of other credible adults. Any other action is folly. Teachers have faced court testimony from student complaining of suspect physical conduct such as these: "a boyfriend-type hug"; "patted my back, over my bra strap"; "held my hand"; "put her arm around my waist"; "patted my hips"; "hugged me too long"; "patted my head"; "bumped into me"; "gave me a backrub." Any teacher with more than a few months in the classroom could attest to the benign nature of such daily events. On the other hand, the end result of such physical demonstrations of affection may be that you will be expected to explain such actions in court. Explaining that you show such physical demonstrations to all students will only make matters worse. You never know what a simple hug is communicating to a student. You may be thinking "positive support." The student may be thinking "returned affection." Worse yet, for the student who has endured past physical or sexual abuse, such physical demonstrations bring terrible memories. In the face of such misunderstanding and potential for harm, why not curb your own behavior?

5. *Do not place yourself in an automobile alone with students.* You should not transport students in your own vehicle, simply because of the liability risk.

6. *Do not give out your home or cell phone number to students.* This is perhaps the most common mistake made by first-year teachers. Inexperienced teachers want to show students the best of intentions and demonstrate their real-world concern for student achievement. Their phone number, home or cell, provides a way for students to reach them to ask questions or express concerns. In reality, phone conversations often become opportunities for personal messages. Calls may have many listeners. Teachers who allow phone calls to their home or cell provide enterprising students with an opportunity for risky personal communication.

7. *Do not give out your personal email address.* Students of all ages feel very comfortable with technology. Many know that instant messaging facilitates email interruption, as long as the targeted person is on line. Teachers find they cannot use their computer without receiving constant obscene messages from multiple anonymous sources. Online chat rooms and "face" sites can be utilized by disgruntled students to post suggestive comments aimed at specific teachers. Remember never to respond to any online notation, regardless of the content. Expecting law enforcement to track down the culprit is a pipe dream; expecting parents to curb computer privileges may be as elusive.

8. *Do not give presents to students.* When teachers hand out jewelry, t-shirts, cards, or personal notes, they find it difficult to explain these actions in court. Juries wonder, "Why would a teacher favor a specific student with a gift unless something was expected in return?" State boards of education and civil courts see this as a quid pro quo, something given for a favor in return. Playing favorites with gifts encourages students to expect a special level of personal influence with the teacher.

9. *Do not attend social events held by students.* Family events such as graduations, weddings, and birthday parties are wonderful events to share with your students, but be wary that they do not result in student-only celebrations. Should you arrive to find that all participants are under age, you must leave immediately. Attending a party given by students sets the scene for rampant rumors of inappropriate teacher actions.

10. *Do not invite students to your home.* Year-end parties or sleepovers offer students a view of teachers' personal lives. Remember, everything that happens in your domicile is your responsibility and may in fact become the basis for an allegation of sexual misconduct or student injury. Should you employ a student to babysit in your home, be sure there are plenty of safeguards for taking the student home. At no time should you be alone with the student.

11. *Do not lend money to students.* Every teacher has at some time lent lunch money to hungry students. Often teachers do not expect repayment; unfortunately, some have been repaid with an allegation that they gave the money to a student to purchase special favors from them.

12. *Do not write personal notes to students.* Please remember, comments on graded papers are not covered in this advice. Personal letters to students are forbidden. What reason could a teacher have to begin and continue a personal correspondence outside class? Parents and community members will think the worst.

13. *Do not post student pictures in your room with suggestive titles or captions.* Labeling a student the "Cutest Girl in Town" or "My Special Girls" will mislead every student in your class. If you enjoy posting student pictures, do so without captions.

14. *Don't allow students to call you "Mom" or "Dad."* Although the title may be a result of true affection permission to use a nickname for you encourages students to step over the professional barrier that must be present in every classroom.

15. *School bus seating should be adult with adult.* Many allegations of teacher sexual misconduct have been fueled by an adult sitting in a close-quarters bus seat with a student. Students in the rear of the bus rarely misbehave when two adults are sitting in adjacent seats. If there is only one adult on the bus, he must take an entire seat.

16. *Do not take students home from school.* Taking a student home poses its own problems. How do you know the house is actually the student's residence? How do you know the house is safe for the student? Who is home to receive the student? Is there any potential for an assault on you? You must call the local police to take the student home. This action may seem hardhearted, but it is the only legal action you can take to ensure student safety (and your continued employment). The police will safely escort the student to the door. They will confirm that this is the correct residence and inquire if there is a responsible party to supervise the student.

17. *Be aware that field trips that include an overnight stay pose problematic situations.* Entering a hotel or motel room where students are housed is also not a good idea. Supervision by certified personnel during extended field trips should be completed by teams of teachers, rather than by one person checking rooms alone. Lock-ins in any setting pose a dangerous risk for teachers who may be in the wrong place at the wrong time. Prior planning for staffing should see to it that there are male and female instructors along on the trip. Male teachers who deal with female students quickly find that there is a double standard in education. Female teachers seem to have much more leeway in supervising students than male teachers. Perhaps because of their association with the maternal role, female teachers may supervise girls and boys in a gender-neutral manner.

18. *Do not date a student, even a former student.* Remember, sexual abuse of minors has no statute of limitation in many states. Several court cases have been initiated 10 to 30 years after the alleged event. A minor can never legally give consent for a sexual relationship.

19. *Don't give a student an extended hall pass to move freely around the building.* Writing out semester-long passes encourages students to feel they have a special relationship with you. They also feel a bit more important than their peers because they enjoy your attention and trust. That semester-long hall pass could equally appear to be a ticket to a tryst. Take the time to write out a specific pass for a specific day and time, and note the reason. You may need the notation to prompt your memory in case of an allegation. Take up and keep all expired hall passes.

20. *Mentoring relationships must maintain professional boundaries.* When school districts formally pair teachers with at-risk kids, the potential exists for eroding professional barriers. The practice of getting to know students and their families is a good idea; taking students into your personal life is a bad idea. When establishing a mentoring relationship, teachers are expected to keep a positive, supporting relationship that is clearly aboveboard, on a professional standing, and beyond reproach.

21. *Always have all students due to arrive and depart at the same time.* Extracurricular activities often take place in an empty school. When a single student arrives early or stays after others are gone, the odds improve that an allegation of misconduct may arise.

22. *Save all student notes.* Although you should never read a student note out loud in the classroom, you should never throw away any student-student notes. The best

practice is to read the note and document the date and the student's name. Keep the note until the end of the year.

23. *Do not post cartoons that could appear sexist or demeaning.* Times have changed. Posting notes that ridicule males or females sets a negative tone in the classroom and encourages students to mimic such behavior.

24. *Do not allow students to call you by your first name.* No matter how informal the setting, you must keep a professional distance from your students. When students attempt to call you by anything but your last name, correct them immediately.

25. *When planning any off-campus activity, include male and female supervisors.* Even if you invite a very dependable parent, you will need to ensure that girls are being supervised by a female and boys are being supervised by males.

26. *Do not allow inappropriate joking between students.* Federal mandates restrict public comments made in a sexually harassing tone. Regardless of whether you join in the conservation, you are responsible for immediately stopping sexual joking, flirting, or actions. Use your leadership to immediately stop the situation. Your silence in such a situation implies your consent.

27. *Do not share information about one student with another.* Maintaining confidentiality is of the utmost importance.

28. *Do not make a professional referral to a clinical counselor or physician without the parents' approval.* The custodial parent is the only legal entity who can approve medical or psychiatric care for a minor.

29. *Do not use physical force to correct students.* Teachers are expected to keep control of their anger and emotions. Many schools employ security personnel, trained and insured, to handle such a situation.

30. *Do not leave students unattended, and be sure all activities, including independent seatwork, are safely supervised at all times.*

31. *Arrive on time for all assigned duties.* This applies to recess, hallway, or bus supervision.

32. *Consider safety issues in every class activity.* Hot pans, candles, sharp objects, and shaky displays can contribute to a negligence suit by students who are harmed in avoidable accidents.

33. *Do not attempt to treat a medical condition unless certified to do so.*

34. *Do not send students on teacher errands away from formal supervision at any time.* Allowing students to leave campus to get treats, buy materials, or go home without parental approval places the teacher at liability for allegations of negligence and places the student in harm's way.

VOICES FROM THE FIELD—DRAWING THE LINE WITH STUDENTS

Jenny Tripses, PhD

Teaching is a noble profession. The chance to positively influence young people and to help them to acquire the skills, knowledge, and character they will carry with them all their lives is an incredible opportunity, but also a challenge. I believe it's critical for all beginning teachers to enter into teaching with a combined sense of idealism and realism—idealism, because good teachers have a profound effect on their students, and realism, because there are negative, indeed toxic, influences in education that can turn idealism into forces that tarnish the teacher, the students, and others around them. I hope that you want to hang onto your idealism even as you face the challenges.

The first challenge involves the nature of teaching. Teaching is very hard work. Don't let anyone fool you about that. Good teaching takes dedication and commitment. And, although things do get simpler with experience, the actual time and energy required to do your best remain for teachers with 2 or 30 years of experience. So it's important to know well the craft of teaching and to realize that there is always more to learn. You don't nurture lifelong learning in your students unless you take your own learning very seriously. One of the ways that you can transition more quickly from a novice teacher to an experienced pro (who still works pretty hard but is able to step back more often and enjoy a sense of accomplishment) is to conquer classroom management. One of the best resources on classroom management is the book *How to Be an Effective Teacher: The First Days of School*, by Harry Wong and Rosemary Wong. The book is chock-full of ideas for managing your classroom. Even after 33 years' experience in teaching and administration, I find helpful ideas in the Wongs' book that I can use in my graduate classes. My hope is that you will get your hands on a copy of the book or another one like it and refer to it often.

The second challenge I present to you is to decide here and now what kind of teacher you intend to be. I'm talking here about professionalism. Sadly, there are teachers out there who somehow along the way lost their idealistic sense of making a difference in the lives of their students. They have lost sight of their reasons for going into teaching. These are the harpers and complainers who arrive at the last possible moment each morning, rush out the door in the afternoon the minute they are contractually allowed to do so, and spend every available minute allowed them in between in the teachers' lounge complaining about the students, parents, and administration. If you decided to go into teaching in order to make a difference in the lives of your students, you have to decide right now that you are not going to become one of their camp. This is not optional. Either you're one of the complainers or you're not. Trust me, they'll do their best to get you on their side. Be aware that these kinds of influences will be alive and well in your first teaching assignment. I advise you to use the strategy you used to stay out of trouble in high school: "Just say no!" You don't want to be a part of that kind of negativism and soul-nagging behavior. You've worked too hard to be an outstanding teacher to succumb to attitudes that blame and shame.

So how do you go about becoming the best teacher you can be? I believe it's very important to carefully look at the experienced teachers in your building and to seek out the ones you admire. You can tell these teachers by the way they talk about their students (and parents). There is a level of respect given to all students, the challenging ones as well as the more accomplished. These teachers don't have time to complain. You can tell these teachers by their appreciation for the opportunity to continuously learn with their students. You can tell these teachers by the way they reflect upon their classrooms.

They'll talk with you about ideas they've tried in the classroom, what worked, what didn't, and why. They'll take a sincere interest in you as a teaching professional—that's very different from taking an interest in you as a potential ally in the cause of whining and complaining. You can tell professional teachers because they take responsibility for fixing problems as they occur, and they'll invite you to be a part of the solution.

I wish you all the best in your career as a teacher. You have chosen well. Teaching *is* a noble profession for those who decide early on to be the best teacher possible each and every day. Notice that I didn't say perfect. Teaching is hard work. Teaching is also very rewarding work for those who work hard to learn their craft, realizing that learning never stops in the classroom for the teacher as well as the students. Teaching is rewarding for those who consciously seek out other professional teachers to learn together. Good luck, noble teacher.

CHAPTER 3

Drawing the Line with Parents

Key Concepts

Family Educational Rights and Privacy Act
Privileged communication
Standardized testing
Custodial parent
Grade retention
Grade promotion
Think sheet
Teacher-centered conference
Student-centered conference
Student-led conference
No Child Left Behind
Foster care
Placement plan
Assault
Battery
Pupil Protection Rights Amendment

This chapter will:

1. Define the three major types of parent conferences found in schools.
2. Provide a list of materials that should be included in each conference.
3. Describe the legal implications of parents' academic decisions.
4. Suggest important topics to be covered in parent conferences.

Parents File Suit to Limit Administrators Authority to Transfer Students
Parents File Suit to Keep Student Information Out of Hands of Private Company
Parents File Suit for Negligence by Teacher
Parents Recover IDEA Consultant Fees
Parents Successful after IDEA Claim, Receive Attorney Fees
School District Liable in Harassment Case
Parents Sue to Block Diversity Training
Parents Sue District for Inaction on Bullying
Michigan District Embroiled in Dispute over Bible Class
Student Allowed to Sue District over First Amendment Rights
Parent Files Complaint Alleging Retaliation
Georgia Parents Oppose Evolution Disclaimer
Pennsylvania Parents File Suit over Truancy Charges
Parents Sue District over Alleged Abuse

This is just a sampling of the stormy legal waters that can be found by a simple check of one professional site on the Internet.[1] Civil suits, filed by parents, run the continuum from allegations of sexual harassment by teachers to charges of lack of supervision of students. In the past, parents have brought suit for violations of civil rights; religious discrimination; violation of compulsory attendance laws; negligence, child endangerment, and neglect of duty of care; breach of contract; poor curriculum design and selection; due process violations, and violations of freedom of speech, among others. In fact, the number of law cases involving parents and school districts has increased in the past 15 years more than any other kind of civil suits.

Parents can be a teacher's best advocate or worse enemy. Developing strong home-school connections is an art crafted after many years of communication and involvement. The key descriptors for parental communication are these:

1. *Professional*: All communication must rise to the level of competent professionalism. That is, it must be informative, accurate, and timely in nature.
2. *Proactive*: Many student problems could have been solved when the problem was still a small one. Allowing small problems to become large through simple neglect is a poor practice for education professionals.
3. *Positive*: All communications must be positive in tone to be effective. Admittedly, many student behavior problems simply have no good news connected with them, but the educator must still measure words with professional politeness, respect, and courtesy. Educators will find that when these three descriptors are present, communication between teacher and parents is optimized.

One elementary school teacher wrote a letter to parents explaining why final grades for the year were not available for her students:

Yesterday, I cried and slept and slept and slept and cried, unmotivated to complete your child's report card as planned. You know your child best. Please complete the final quarter of the report card. How does it feel to you?[2]

This teacher has certainly failed the test of positive, proactive, and professional communication to parents.

HOW DO EFFECTIVE TEACHERS PREPARE
FOR PARENT CONFERENCES?

Impromptu parent conferences may happen in the school hallway, at an "open house" visit, or during an extracurricular event. Impromptu conferences set the stage for tragedy when critical information, meant to be said in private, is repeated in public. Such conferences must never occur at local stores, social events, or sporting events. The only correct forum for any parent conference is within the school walls. Teachers are reminded to be in compliance with FERPA regulations regarding the sharing of information about students. Only teachers or school staff who have some professional need for the information may be consulted. Be sure to be aware of the FERPA requirements and of the federal Pupil Protection Rights Amendment (PPRA), which are discussed later in this chapter.

Formal parent conferences test the professionalism of the teacher as well as fulfill the teacher's legal responsibility to keep parents aware of the academic progress of the student. Individual Educational Plans (IEP), as mandated in special-education programs, require annual meetings to review student progress.[3] Many schools plan formal parent conferences twice a year—fall and spring. Time frames for parent conferences vary depending on the school district. This is a time (usually 15–25 minutes) for teachers and parents to sit down together to review and evaluate student work and academic progress, as well as to plan future work goals. Teachers must be well prepared for the brief conference—much has to be said in a relatively short amount of time. Teachers who spend precious minutes searching around for a slip of paper give the impression that they are "flying by the seat of their pants." The only acceptable behavior that will build the confidence of the parents fosters the image of a competent, caring professional.

Key materials that must be at arm's length during academic conferences include the following:

- *Grade book or a hard copy of an electronic grade sheet* (i.e., E-Class, Gradekeeper, Excel). Your grade book will help you quickly check individual grades, work submitted late, specific subject grades, patterns in achievement, and missing assignments. Be sure the grade book is not shared with parents in such a way that the parents may be able to view the grades of other students. This is a clear violation of the privacy of student educational records. If you must share the sheet of grades, be sure to do so in such a way that only one specific student record is visible.

- *Attendance records.* Such records offer a unique look at student persistence. Many schools now have electronic attendance programs that easily keeps track of teacher-entered information. Be sure to print out the attendance record or have clear notes about chronic tardiness. Such information can provide key insights about student progress. Only by looking for patterns in attendance or tardiness can the teacher ask pertinent questions during the conference. For example, many students, especially in low-income areas, must wait for parents to get home to assume care of younger siblings before the student can come to school. Many older students help prepare their younger siblings for the school day. The oldest child is expected to make lunches, change the little one's clothes, and get backpacks ready. The oldest child then rushes to beat the tardy bell. Unbelievably, some students are not expected by parents to attend school on Mondays or Fridays or on the days before or after any school holiday. Perhaps a student feels ill and goes to the clinic at the same time every day; attendance records accumulated over a semester will show the many hours of instruction missed in one subject—which may help to explain failing grades in that subject. Finally, secondary students may have figured out which teachers actually keep accurate attendance and which do not. Teachers who do not keep attendance accurately give students an opportunity to leave campus undetected.

- *Work samples/testing results.* Parents are interested in seeing actual examples of their child's progress and want to see how those compare with the work of others in the same class. Teachers should have three examples to show for each assignment. Teachers should have an "A" exemplary paper, a "C" minimum-passing paper, and an "F" failing paper for the same assignment. Be sure to remove all personal information from the paper. In compliance with FERPA, no identifying information can be left on the papers to protect the identity of the student worker. When parents see the papers and compare them to their own child's work, many of their questions will be answered. Teacher must also be well versed in the explanation of pertinent standardized test scores. When parents ask about stanines and coefficients, the teacher should be able to guide them back to the most important aspects of the testing results for the academic progress of their child. Trying to remember the definitions of all statistical testing terms or relying on what was learned years ago in college courses will only sound silly and give the impression the teacher knows very little. In sum, know the information you must convey, and don't try to fake answers to parents' questions.

- *Behavior notes.* The notes teachers have made regarding the daily interaction and behaviors of the student are the teacher's private observation *until shared.* At that point, the notes are part of the student's educational records and will be given protection in a court of law. The rule, simply stated, is this: if the notes are shared for any reason, they become an official record. Teachers must be quite tactful in what they write, include only observable behaviors, and keep the notation neutral in tone. Teachers might make a copy for the parents to take home and discuss with their student.

- *Classroom rules.* Since the 1980s, Lee Canter's Assertive Discipline plan has encouraged teachers to formulate and post three to five easily understood classroom rules at the start of the school year.[4] The first days of the school year then are spent in discussion and practice of classroom or schoolwide rules for student behavior. Being quite sure that students understand what is expected of them allows a teacher to be proactive when crafting an environment for learning. When parents understand and support the classroom rules, there is a basis for continuity in student discipline. A good practice for teachers is to have a copy of the classroom rules signed by all three stakeholders—teachers, students, and parents. A copy should be kept close at hand during parent conferences.

- *School handbook.* Many schools have developed a daily planner format for the school handbook. The handbook includes information about dress codes, bathroom passes, homework numbers, Web sites, school phone numbers, and bus transportation schedules. A copy of the handbook is essential when you need to refer parents to a specific rule or policy.

- *School calendar.* This resource facilitates a look at upcoming events, school holidays, or early dismissal dates.

- *Seating chart.* Having a seating chart handy helps to clarify the immediate context for "homework helpers"—classmates who can help with make-up work. The chart may also help to identify any potential discipline issues. Every teacher knows that a constant talker sitting beside a long-time friend is a bad combination.

- *Lesson-plan books.* Teachers plan instruction for every day. The process is ongoing. Parents may ask spur-of-the-moment questions about the length of a unit or when a task was assigned. Such information may be difficult to recall without a written record of pages, question numbers, tests, and homework due dates.

- *Text books.* Teachers should have class texts stacked to the side of the conference area. Often students lose books, then take a classmate's to use as their own. When parents are afforded a gentle visual reminder, teachers can count on the book being found "under the bed" or in the car trunk and being returned to the classroom.

- *Notepaper/conference sheet.* When a teacher takes notes during a conference the parent gains confidence that the teacher will not forget the main points discussed and the agreements reached. Using a standard format will help the teacher add in specific information. Notes should include the date and time of the conference; who attended; topics covered; timelines set for the next conference; and student support materials like homework sheet or behavior contract.

- *Homework sheet.* Occasionally teachers need to provide an incentive for students to write down homework assignments and due dates. The age-old homework sheet predated the modern planner or Palm Pilot. Today, schools may provide all homework assignments via phone line or on a Web site. If teachers are called upon to resort to twentieth-century methods—paper copy—be sure to follow through in your daily checking for completed assignments and notations.

- *Your professional card.* Many schools now provide teachers with business cards emblazoned with the district logo, district number, and essential phone numbers for contact during school hours. Keep these ready. Parents who have many children attending the same school can easily become confused as to each teacher's room numbers and name.

Being prepared is half the battle; teachers must also display the highest professional behavior throughout the conference. Additional ideas include these:

- Invite both parents.
- Make the contact early in the year—positive, proactive, professional.
- Allow enough time for the conference, stay on time—do not make parents wait in the hall.
- Be ready for questions.
- Plan ahead—start positive, give information, and end on a positive tone.
- Greet parents as close to the entrance as possible.
- Be sure you use the correct name (it is completely acceptable to ask).

- Don't sit behind a physical barrier. Stay out of isolated areas. Stay in clear sight lines of other faculty.
- Be specific in your comments. Be sure to have the student's name correct.
- Ask for the parent's opinion.
- Suggest a course of action.
- Focus on student strengths and solutions.
- Be a responsive listener—give positive feedback in everything done or said.
- Summarize aloud.
- Take notes.
- Plan to meet again if necessary, and have an appointment calendar ready.
- Be on time and stay on time throughout the conference day.
- Dress for success; be sure your appearance says "professional."

The content of parent conferences may include the following:

- *Initial Introductions.* Remember, teachers must be sure they are speaking with the custodial parents, not a babysitter, sibling, or friend of the parent. Custodial parents have total legal responsibility for the child in their full-time care. If the adult attending is not the custodial parent, you must delay the conference until the actual parents can attend. In case of families with limited English proficiency, an interpreter may attend. A word to the wise—should the interpreter be an older sibling, the parent may not be getting the exact information the teacher is saying. The sibling may have ulterior motives for changing the conference content or intent.
- *Student behavior.* Be clear and precise. Weigh the words before they are said. Parents may take a decidedly defensive tone even when no insult was intended.
- *Student absences.* Be sure parents know if there is a school district or state regulation that limits the number of absences above which a student is retained. Families that move from state to state may not know of such guidelines.
- *Upcoming class projects or field trips.* The parent conference may be the only time for parents to sign permission slips. Every teacher has students who must stay behind on field trip days because no parent was available to sign a release for travel to the destination. Class project due dates can be placed in the parent's personal calendar. Every parent has experienced the eleventh-hour panic of attempting to finish a three-week project in a few hurried hours.
- *Classroom rules.* Cover them briefly. It is a good idea to have the rules written as a contract with three signature blanks—one for teacher, one for student, and one for parents.
- *Achievement levels.* Most parents are familiar with American-style grade levels. If test results can be placed in a context of "on grade level," "below grade level," or "above grade level," communication is enhanced.
- *Opportunities for specialized education.* Parents may be interested in tutoring for their children or in finding homework helpers from a higher grade. Additionally, the teacher may believe the child needs eyeglasses. Be very careful in "diagnosing" learning problems. Always give any recommendation in the most general terms, for

example, "Perhaps an evaluation for additional tutoring will help provide the support needed to succeed." Teachers may not recommend specific resource agents, such as counselors, optometrists, or physicians, by name.

- *Family changes.* All families go through good and bad times. This is the teacher's opportunity to identify any changes in the family, such as the death of a sibling or parent, that may impact learning in the classroom.

- *Grade retention or promotion.* Usually during in the spring conference, the parent may be given advance warning of the possibility that the student will be retained at the end of the academic year. For example, a second-grade student may need to stay in second grade for the next school year. This is a very difficult topic, and the best advice is to include an administrator in the conference if the potential for retention exists.

A teacher may request that a parent conference focus on a disciplinary or student behavior issue. This type of conference is different from an academic conference. Behavior concerns must be dealt with on an event-by-event basis as quickly after the behavior as possible, certainly by the next day. Keep all behavior notes and all student notes. Using a Think Sheet facilitates a record of the infraction in the student's own words.

The use of a Think Sheet, as outlined in Lee Canter's discipline program, is essential for obtaining a written record of the event from the student's point of view.[5] Immediately after the event, separate the student from the group, and have the student write the answers to the following three questions:

What happened?
Why did it happen?
What should have happened if everyone were following the classroom rules?

The process of writing immediately after the infraction has a threefold purpose. First, the teacher has a record of the events in the student's own handwriting, before the story changes to accommodate a sympathetic parent. Second, the actual physical and mental effort of writing seems to defuse the emotional response to the event. Third, the Think Sheet allows teachers to handle the infraction at a more convenient time for the instructional flow.

WHAT ARE THE MOST COMMON TYPES OF PARENT CONFERENCES?

No matter where teachers practice their craft, parent conferences will fall into one of three categories.

Why Use a Teacher-Centered Conference?

In this very formal type of parent conference, teachers are in control of every aspect of the conference time. Usually such conferences are given midway in the first grading period and again midway in the last grading period, and they are commonly termed fall and spring conferences. Teachers schedule the conference into distinct time frames of perhaps 15 to 25 minutes. Sometimes parents may choose the time frame that best fits their personal schedules. Sometimes parents have no choice and are assigned a time to be present in the classroom. Parents who work during the school day are usually accommodated with evening conferences for one or two nights.

Teacher-centered conferences are by far the most common format for parent conferences for several good reasons. Teachers set the tone and pace of the conference. Teachers decide the topics to be covered and plan the location of the conference. The teacher meets the parents, shares all conference materials, and provides a summary at the end of the conference period. If parents cannot attend the scheduled conference, they simply miss the opportunity. No make-up time is offered, because the teacher must return to his duties as instructor.

Positive aspects of teacher-centered conferences include these:

- Such traditional formats are comfortable for both parent and teacher.
- Materials can be prepared in advance and personalized per student.
- Student conduct or behavior, as well as academics, can be discussed.
- Professional settings facilitate professional behavior by all parties.
- Privacy concerns are protected because admission to the conference is strictly controlled.
- School administrators know and favor traditional formats.
- Teams of teachers can utilize the format very effectively.
- Thanks to the one-to-one setting, parents may feel more at ease about confiding in teachers regarding family events or emergencies that may impact the student.
- Teachers can obtain signatures on permission slips for upcoming school events, rather than risk sending the paperwork home.

Negative aspects of teacher-centered conferences include the following:

- Because of the participants' isolation in a classroom, hostile parents may pose a safety concern.
- Students get the feeling they are being talked about, rather than being able to participate in the decision-making process.
- Parents may want to initiate such conferences in the context of an informal setting such as an afterschool activity or a chance meeting in the school hallway.
- Teachers are held responsible by the parents for explaining why student progress is poor. Teachers may feel the need to explain the student's lack of motivation with regard to missed homework assignments or poor grades on projects.
- Because of the brief timeframe, the conference may feel rushed, because more parents are waiting in the hallway.

- Parents may feel intimidated by teams of teachers dispensing bad news about their child.
- Conferences can become bogged down on discipline issues and fail to cover academics.
- Teachers are seen as the final authority in all academic and behavior decisions.

What Are Student-Centered Conferences?

In this second most common type, the student participates as an equal partner with teacher and parents. Although the conference is still primarily planned by the teacher, students have direct input during the conference and participate in any decision making or goal setting at end of the conference.

Positive aspects of the student-centered conference include the following:

- Students have direct input in all information shared and decisions.
- Behavior problems and/or poor academic progress reports can be directly explained by the student.
- Students may bring materials to the conference they would like to share, but primary emphasis is placed on teacher-selected materials.
- Scheduling is very much the same as with the teacher-centered conferences. Teachers schedule the parents and students to confer for 15 to 25 minute.
- Traditional formats are only slightly changed; administrators feel comfortable with the familiar format, as well.
- Parent-student interaction can be observed by the teachers. It is very interesting to watch family dynamics. There are families where the children are clearly in control.
- Parents are more likely to question the student about failing grades, rather than the teacher.
- Student honesty levels are highly increased because a "Teacher says/but I say" response is short-circuited when the teacher and student are both present.

Negative aspects of the student-centered conference include the following:

- Students may be frightened about a bad report and "clam up."
- Parents may shift into a defensive "bravado" mode when discipline issues are brought up.
- In cases of parents with limited English proficiency, students who translate for their parents may not be accurate in their choice of wording.
- Students may agree to a strategy for remediation in front of the parents but not follow though once the conference is done.
- Many families require older children to care for younger ones. The need for older siblings to babysit during the parent conference prevent them from attending with their parents. Perhaps students have to keep an eye on younger children, who are present in the classroom, as the teacher is leading the conference. This situation is not a positive

one. The concept of "school as a safe place" requires the environment—the location of the conference area—to be prepared for little children, even if the setting is a high school science lab.[6]

Why Use Student-Led Conferences?

The least common parent conference format is the student-led conference. Upper elementary grades and middle schools often implement student-led conferences. The age of the child permits them to take over control of the parent conference. In this format, no student behavior problems are discussed, and all conversation revolves around academics. If behavior concerns exist, a separate traditional conference must be scheduled. The student-led conference allows teachers to schedule several parent conferences in the same 25-minute time slot. For example, each corner of the classroom can contain a table and chairs for conferences. That permits four conferences to go on at the same time. Certainly this gives parents more time slots from which to select when the conference day arrives. Parental work schedules make it hard for parents to attend the conference. Some parents may lose wages if they come, while others may need handicap modifications to attend. Many states have statues that require any employer with more than 50 employees to provide paid or unpaid leave for parents who must attend school parent conference during their usual work hours.[7]

Each family conference begins the same way. That is, students give their parents a tour of the room, pointing out important projects, assignments that have been posted, and their own desk area. Then families move to a corner and sit to allow the student to complete the conference. The remainder of the conference is done according to a script. For example, "Mom, this is my Language Arts journal. I have earned 5 'Bs' and 1 'A' in my daily journal." Or again, "Dad, this semester I worked hardest on the science experiment project. Here are the grades I earned." Students read their specific answers to questions about the academic work, share success and failures, and report their grades in each subject. Students write their own learning goals and share those with the parent. During this process, the teacher circulates around the room, stopping to make brief comments about the schoolwork highlighted. The conference ends with the parent signing the script to indicate that the conference was successfully completed.

Positive aspects of the student are these:

- Students truly own this conference. They compose the script with the teacher's guidance.
- Parents find this type of conference very attractive and comfortable.
- Multiple conferences can be scheduled simultaneously.
- No danger is present in the classroom for any of the stakeholders.

- Student work is the centerpiece of the conference.
- Goals are set between parent and student.
- Students must answer fully for their school effort or lack of it.
- Portfolio assessment fits this format perfectly.
- If the parents cannot or do not attend, conferences can take place at home or with other school personnel, such as an administrator or counselor.
- Parents find this type of conference less intimidating than talking with the teacher alone.
- Students whose parents who cannot attend may take the script home and have the conference there.
- Time constraints are less restrictive; families may move at their own pace through the script.
- For some children, the conference affords them 25 uninterrupted minutes of parental attention for perhaps the only time in several weeks.

Negative aspects of student-led conference include the following:

- Preparation for the conference takes several weeks, as student prepare their scripts and have them approved by their teachers.
- Team conferences with several teachers are impossible to schedule.
- Students may not mention key areas of information or become bogged down in less significant issues.
- Teachers have less time for giving information about upcoming events.
- No private information can be shared because of the proximity of other parties.
- Teachers may not get to see extended periods of parent/student interaction.
- School administrators may not feel this is a "real" parent conference.
- Parents may not schedule an additional conference if they have questions or if behavior concerns exist.
- This type of conference cannot be used to discuss a retention decision or diagnostic testing for special-education placement.

Student-led conferences are the newest formats in many elementary, middle, and high schools, and many school districts are beginning to phase in the process over many years, one grade at a time.

WHAT ARE THE LEGAL ISSUES FOR PARENT CONFERENCES?

Ensuring the Safety of Teaching Professionals

National statistics regarding involving teachers who are threatened or injured by parents continue to increase.[8] The teacher who has secluded the parent conference area at the back of a classroom or behind a partition may indeed be at risk for assault and battery. Assault occurs when one is put in fear of harm by the actions of another; no physical contact is necessary.[9] Battery involves physical contact by another in a rude and angry manner. Most states hold assault or battery committed against any school personnel to be a felony offense.[10] For example, Florida assigns the level of a third-degree felony to assault or battery committed against a school employee.[11] Criminal charges are the natural result.

School administrators must never expect teachers *not to file* charges against parents who have committed or threatened assault and/or battery. Under district policy, teachers may be required to present a written complaint to the school administrator within three days of the incident.[12] Administration support for teachers who have experienced threatening or abusive behavior is key in establishing a safe environment for school employees—certified or noncertified.

Must Teachers Endure Verbal Abuse?

Freedom of speech does not allow for all manner of speech. Teachers conducting parent conferences may experience verbal abuse from irate parents. No constitutional protections are afforded to vulgar, obscene, or threatening speech. Parents are not free to say anything to anyone. Parents who show a pattern of inappropriate behavior toward school staff, school administrators, or board members will have their right to be on school property limited by court injunction for harassing behavior or by a court-ordered restraining order (even if the behavior is evidenced in a single episode).[13] Disgruntled parents who make false claims, such as child abuse, against teachers may also face legal repercussions for defamation of character.[14] Finally, the No Child Left Behind legislation is meant to provide "teachers, principals and other school professionals the tools they need to undertake reasonable actions to maintain order, discipline, and an appropriate educational environment."[15] Federal mandates set limits on teacher liability and protect teachers and school districts in state and federal court suits filed by parties suing for economic or noneconomic loss caused by negligence on the part of school personnel. The act sets monetary limits for any damages and preempts state statutes that are different from NCLB (Section 2365).

Case in Point

Independent School District No. 381 v. Olson, No. C9-00-888, 2001 WL 32807 (Minn. Ct. App. 2001)

A parent who was upset about scheduling choices made for his son by school personnel yelled at several teachers and shouted that he planned to return to the school in five minutes with witnesses. Although he did not return to the school, he did write a threatening letter to the principal. The court found that this parent had displayed harassing behavior and restricted his future access to the school.

Talk It Over

A parent is upset over having to replace a textbook lost by her child. The parent uses the issue to belittle and threaten an elementary school teacher. The building administrator expects the teacher to accept the parent's angry threats and allegations without responding in any way. The book is found in the next few weeks under the student's bed. No apology is ever given. Did the school administrator overstep her authority to expect the teacher to stand the onslaught of the angry parent without reply? If the teacher spoke up, would that have been an act of insubordination?

Best-Practice Overview

Teachers should strive to keep a positive tone in all written and verbal communication. Regardless of a teacher's professional demeanor, the presence of angry parents is a perennial possibility. Do not get into shouting matches with parents. Simply excuse yourself and leave the area. There is no expectation in any collective-bargaining agreement or state statute that teachers must accept personal insults or uncensored criticism from parents. If parents are abusive or begin to curse during a phone conversation, simply ask the parent to call the front office to schedule a parent conference at a later time, and then hang up. Do not accept home phone calls from parents, and do not allow abusive emails. Make such interactions known to the school administrator. Keep documentation of all such episodes, and expect support from district officials. Forgiving and forgetting such rude displays allows a bullying parent to continue such behavior with impunity. Your report may save another colleague from such a scene. Always, in every communication, model courteous behavior by being positive, proactive, and professional.

MAY A THIRD PARTY ATTEND THE CONFERENCE?

In the event a parent conference has the potential to become negative in tone, teachers should invite a neutral third party to attend the conference. The right to privacy of education records will not inhibit a third party, a certified school employee, from attending a discussion of student achievement.[16] Administrators or quasi-administration personnel, such as counselors, should sit in on parent conferences that may become volatile in tone. Teachers should be sure to give the third party a short overview of the format for the conference, plan a secure area for the conference, and introduce the additional member to the parents upon their arrival.

Case in Point

Dawkins v. Billingsley, 69 Okla. 259, 172 P. 69 (1918)

Privileged communication, as protected by state statues, protects statements made in the doctor-patient relationship. But privilege will not be extended to teachers if the statement was made in malice. For example, a teacher noted that a student was "ruined by tobacco and whiskey." Clearly, comments made by any party in a student conference must remain professional.

Talk It Over

A teacher who attended a parent conference as a third party began to share information in the teacher's lounge about the student's mother, who worked as a stripper in a local bar. The principal noted this in the teacher's yearly evaluation as a breach of professional behavior. Fair to the teacher or not?

Best-Practice Overview

In the event a teacher must invite a third party to a parent conference, select someone at an administrative level or a teacher who has the student in his classroom at the time. Do not select a friend on the faculty who might be considered strong "moral support" but who in fact has had no interaction with the student in an instructional setting.

WHAT ARE STUDENT PRIVACY ISSUES?

One is reminded of the World War II saying "Loose lips sink ships." Certainly, as friendships develop, parent conferences may become too informal. Any information said in haste regarding other students in the class, grades earned by other students, parents of other students, or disciplinary situations of other students can and will be considered a violation of those students' privacy. Schools may not release or provide written information about another student without parental signed consent. If parents have a full view of the grade book, other students' files, or notations in student documentations, their wandering eyes will see information meant to be private. If that information is shared, the school will be at fault.

Mentioned in Article IV of the U.S. Constitution, security in private papers is a keystone in American law. The bedrock federal mandate for protecting the student's right to privacy in school records is the Family Education Rights and Privacy Act, or FERPA (20 U.S.C. subsection 1232g:34 CFR Part 99).[17] The act applies to all schools that receive funds from the federal government. The act also outlines a right of redress via a federal complaint against any educational provider who violates a student's protected rights under FERPA. Students and their parents have been granted right to access the students entire educational record.

Special privacy issues may be anticipated when teachers hold parent conferences for students who are placed in court-appointed "placement plans." Usually these involve children in foster homes or at custodial-care schools, such as drug rehab or behavior modification clinics. All documents shared at the conference must be copied and those copies provided to the court-appointed guardian or caseworker attending the conference, to be entered in the child's case file. They become the property of the state and may be entered into court records. No long-term learning plans are expected (unless the student is being served by special education) because child placements can change on a moment's notice. Although juvenile and family courts do not favor moving children from setting to setting, the reality is that this happens frequently. Moves may be made to keep the child from an abusive parent or at the child's request; children may move into an adoptive family or, in the case of older juvenile children, into independent living settings. Finally, remember that getting parents' signatures or family pictures from children in court placement plans may prove impossible or embarrassing to the child. Teachers should be aware of any foster children in their classes and adjust academic reporting procedures accordingly.

Case in Point

Letter to Forgione, 8 FAB 25 (Family Policy Compliance Office 2005)

A high school routinely provides information to a company that supplies cheerleading squads with supplies and services. That company asks for specific information about students with disabilities who are involved in cheerleading. The school agrees to provide this information, even though it is more detailed than information contained in the school directory.

Talk It Over

A high school mistakenly distributes a complete listing of senior class members' names, giving their class rank and their ACT/SAT scores. The parents of those students who rank low on the scale file suit for violation of FERPA. The high school counselors apologize to the entire class. The parents continue the suit, alleging irreparable harm. Can a teacher simply make a poor decision without causing irreparable harm to students?

Best-Practice Overview

All grades that will become part of a student's educational record must be kept private at all times. Private educational "papers" include grades, assessment comments on projects, and graded papers. Covered violations of privacy include posting grades in a hallway or on a bulletin board. Placing unclaimed graded projects in an open area, accessible to anyone, is also a violation of the student's privacy. If you wish to show an "A" paper to another student's parents so that they can compare it with their own child's work, be sure that the example paper has all private information blotted out so that no connection can be made to an individual. Do not give out any student information, even phone numbers, to other students or parents. Do not show videotapes of class performances if the student can be identified by watching the tape (e.g., by a name tag). Do not use another student's name in describing a disciplinary situation. Simply call the other student "a classmate." Do not allow parents of one student to speak privately with another student or provide a phone number so that one parent can speak with another, even if, for example, a student finds a lost jacket and takes it home, telling the teacher, "Just have anyone call my house if this is their jacket." The school principal is best able to decide if a potential violation of exists. The district will expect the building administrator to make the decision, even if she is wrong. Students are guaranteed privacy of their educational records by federal law. Remember, teachers would feel the same way if their doctor, pastor, or counselor shared information about their health and activities with others or displayed private records to the public by posting information in a public office or on a Web site.

DO TEACHERS MAKE HOME VISITS?

Historically, teachers were required to make home visits to the homes of their current students. This was common practice until the 1970s. At that time, many teacher contracts required conducting parent conferences in the student's home at least once a year. Truly, this was an eye-opening experience for many teachers, who saw, for the first time, the environment from which their students came. The author was shocked to find deplorable conditions in many student homes, such as family alcoholism, dirt floors, prostitution, open drug-dealing, use of firearms, and poor health conditions. Veteran teachers know that witnessing the home environment illuminates many factors regarding student health and academic progress. Because of the liabilities faced by school districts (that could not or would not provide personal security for teachers), the practice has almost disappeared. On the other hand, many federal preschool programs still send groups of teachers out to conduct home parent conferences and to observe parent/student interaction within the home. School districts will be held liable for placing teachers in dangerous situations that arise while they are completing their teaching duties.

Workman's compensation claims for teacher injuries sustained while the teacher was performing routine work have been successful.[18] This has been the case even where the teacher suffered a mental breakdown and sued for damages resulting from on-the-job mental stress.[19] For teachers to receive compensation from injuries resulting from school district negligence, the district must require home visits of all teachers and then fail to ensure their safety while they are performing the expected duties. Additional legal remedies include civil suits charging the school district with negligence. Teachers can collect money for damage to property, physical injury (including past and future medical expenses), lost earnings, pain, and emotional distress.[20] Remember, home visits mandated by employment contracts must be completed by the teacher. The teacher may have no choice. The result—if the teacher must go, be sure that all possible safety precautions are taken to avoid injury to the teacher.

Case in Point

Johnson v. Unified School District, 191 A.2nd 897 (Pa. 1963)

A temporary teacher refused to attend an after-school "open house" on the grounds she was not a tenured teacher. The school board ended her employment due to insubordination. The civil court commented that the open house was a significant part of the school program and that parents who had made personal sacrifices to attend had been disappointed by her absence. The court held this teacher to be unfit to continue in her employment.

Talk It Over

A grade school (K-8) principal regularly assigns male teachers to attend and supervise boys' basketball and football games. The male teachers feel that all teachers, not just male teachers, should share such additional duties. The principal feels that male teachers can keep better order in sports situations that involve community members, parents, and students. Should one type of duty be given only to specific teachers?

Best-Practice Overview

Teachers should not transport students to homes for a parent conference at any time. School boards must provide transportation for teachers via school bus or in a school administrator's vehicle. Public transportation will not ensure the safety of teacher or student. In emergency situations, the local police will also provide transportation. Scheduling parent conferences in the student's home is a risky venture—for teachers as well as for school districts. In the event a parent is disabled and cannot attend conferences on campus, the school administrator must agree that it is an appropriate accommodation to move the conference to the home. Administration must also provide safety personnel for the conference to ensure the teacher's well-being. Never go in a group of fewer than three people. At no time leave the group of three during the conference. Any injury to teachers who are conducting a school-approved home conference is covered under state workman's compensation laws.

MAY TEACHERS HAVE CLOSE FRIENDSHIPS WITH PARENTS?

The practice of getting to know students and their families is a good idea; taking students or their family into your personal life is a bad idea. Teachers are admonished that developing friendships with parents of students *presently in their charge* is ill advised. All teachers must curtail their social activities to uphold professional boundaries—even with other teachers and their families (if the child is a student in the teacher's class).[21] Although professionals new to the classroom may feel that such friendships will help to ensure parental support in disciplinary cases, the exact opposite is true. Parents of other students may charge the teacher with favoritism or bias, as well as incompetence. When school districts formally pair teachers with at-risk kids, the potential exists for the erosion of professional barriers. When establishing a mentoring relationship, teachers are expected to keep a positive, supporting relationship that is clearly above board, on a professional standing, and beyond reproach.

Teachers who socialize with parents of current students risk being involved in social situations with underage students. Such episodes can easily lend themselves to allegations of teacher misconduct. Family events such as graduations, weddings, and birthday parties are wonderful events to share with your students, but be careful that they are not student-only celebrations. Should you arrive to find that all participants are under age, you must leave immediately. Attending a party given by students sets the scene for rampant rumors of inappropriate teacher actions.

Students should never be invited to a teacher's home. Year-end parties or sleepovers offer students a view of teachers' personal lives. If teachers wish to have a party, select a public place such as a restaurant, and invite several responsible adults to help with supervision. Remember, everything that happens in your domicile is *your responsibility* and may, in fact, become the basis for an allegation of misconduct or liability for student or parent injury. Should you employ a student to babysit in your home, be sure there are plenty of safeguards for taking the student home. At no time should you be alone with the student.

Finally, many states have bans against public employees accepting gifts. Teachers are regulated under state statutes and professional ethics standards. Certainly, accepting *expensive* gifts from parents would qualify as ethics violations. A *gift* is generally defined as any gratuity, discount, entertainment, hospitality, loan, forbearance, or other tangible or intangible item having monetary value, including but not limited to cash, food, and drink and honoraria for speaking engagements related to the teacher's government employment or position as a school employees or member of a school board. Regulations usually forbid the acceptance of any gift with a cash value of more than $75. The general definition of a "giver" includes one who has interests that may be substantially affected by the performance or nonperformance of the official duties of the member, officer, or employee. State bans against accepting gifts also apply to the teacher's spouse and immediate family. State ethics boards perennially hear cases of teacher misconduct arising from the acceptance of gifts or services offered by parents, such as landscaping, carpet cleaning, house painting, or admission to local entertainments. In the case of teachers, state ethics board may levy an administrative fine of up to $5,000 against violators.[22]

Further, in school districts that enforce "no pass-no play" standards for student athletes, gifts from parents may rise to the level of bribery, in that the benefit sought is continued participation in a sport for their child.

Case in Point

Barcheski v. Board of Education of Grand Rapids Public Schools, 412 N.W. 2d 296 (1987)

According to students, a driver's education teacher invited two girls to a local house party. According to the students, both girls accompanied the teacher to the party, at which they participated in drinking beer and using marijuana. The students reported that the teacher then assaulted one girl on the way to her residence. The teacher stated he had attended the student party with two male friends and that the girls were at the party when he arrived. He further stated that he had given the student a ride home because he was concerned for her wellbeing, since she was intoxicated. No criminal charges were ever filed. The teacher was dismissed from his employment.

Talk It Over

A football coach received a large discount on the purchase of a new car from the parent of one of the team players. The principal of the school made no official response or comment, but several parents of other players felt this was a bribe to ensure additional playtime for the athlete. The parent car dealer held that he had simply used his own ability to negotiate the price of the vehicle to benefit a good teacher and coach. He further pointed out that he had, in the past, given gifts of expensive liquor, vehicles, and electronic equipment—including items of NASCAR clothing—to school administrators. No complaints had ever been lodged about the previous gifts.

Best-Practice Overview

Professional teachers must refrain from developing close relationships with the parents of their current students. "Polite" and "professional" must be the key descriptors for all parent-teacher interaction. Sharing details of parents' personal lives, attending family celebrations, and accepting valuable gifts place a teaching professional on shaky ground in the event of a parent complaint. In the same way, accepting gifts is poor decision making. Jewelry, clothing, or food offered by an appreciative student is certainly tempting, but inappropriate. When students ask what you would like for the holidays or as an end-of-the-year thank-you, always suggest they hand-make something, such as a drawing, a poster, or a decorated t-shirt in school colors. They will be pleased to such see handiwork displayed or worn. Additionally, that keeps all gift values to the level of "remembrances," lacking monetary worth but rich in sentimental value. Remember, friendships with families of fellow teachers may be just as volatile as those outside the profession. Transporting students of other teachers will not release the professional from legal and financial liabilities connected to vehicle accidents, allegations of sexual misconduct, or injury to the child.

WHAT PARENTAL ACADEMIC DECISIONS MUST TEACHERS ACCEPT?

All school boards have formally approved learning standards, curriculum books, and materials for all grade levels. School districts must have a clear, comprehensive policy in place that require a multifaceted review of potential instructional materials prior to their formal selection.[23] The U.S. Supreme Court has clearly said that school districts may establish the content of a course.[24] Justices have also decided that parents do not have an unrestricted right to keep their children from taking required courses.[25]

Curricular choices must be based on the following elements:

1. Teacher-made materials must serve a valid educational purpose.
2. Local school boards have the right well as the responsibility to meet state guidelines, national testing requirements, and local priorities when selecting curriculum materials.
3. Teachers must select instructional strategies matched with content material that is acceptable to their school board and approved by building administrators.
4. Teachers may not use the classroom as a forum for personal politics in keeping with the age, maturity level, and experience level of the students.[26]
5. Teachers must confine their teaching to their area of expertise.
6. The board may prohibit by resolution certain subjects that are considered controversial from being introduced in the classroom. [27]

The local school board functions as an arm of state government. Teachers, as representatives of school boards, are legally held to utilizing specific texts, teaching specific skills, and ensuring that students pass comprehensive testing and meet state standards.

Teachers devise unique and creative ways to teach the skills identified by the state. This age-old process of developing interesting, fresh, exciting, and challenging lesson for students may entice teachers to add timely and relevant materials that lie outside the school board–approved curriculum. Teachers must teach that which has already been approved by the school board or by a committee of educators within the district.

Three factors may quickly converge to make lesson plans controversial: use of nonboard–sanctioned materials, teaching of emotionally volatile issues, and a captive classroom audience. When these three elements merge, the chemistry can become explosive. School board members and administrators do not like controversy.

When teachers sign an employment contract, they are promising to teach the curriculum approved by the school board, without exception.[28] Public school teachers lack academic freedom, unlike university professors, who may choose to augment or delete material in a course as they see fit. Elementary and secondary teachers must fulfill the condition of their continued employment or risk dismissal.

Teachers will be taken to task when class materials irk parents or local citizens—even if the nonsanctioned materials have been used successfully in the past. Such materials may include:

- Reading materials with racial or sexual overtones.
- Adult poetry.
- Movies with ratings of PG or above.
- Materials that use vulgar language (written or spoken).
- Material related to the occult.
- Guest speakers who may share unconventional language or subjects.
- Materials connected to sex education.

When parents complain that materials were inappropriate for the school setting, the administrator will consult the school board policy handbook and the approved curriculum. If the materials are outside the approved selections, teachers will be disciplined. If the materials are within the scope of the curriculum, the situation may still prove troublesome for parents. The school board may then decide to change its recommendation on the basis of parental input, but, if it does not, the teacher stands validated. Finally, teachers may not eliminate any materials that may be offensive to their own ideas. For example, a kindergarten teacher who decided not to teach his students about holiday celebrations because they went against his religious beliefs was required by his employment contract to teach the subject matter, regardless of his personal views. The court responded to this teacher this way: "education cannot be left to individual teachers to teach the way they please."[29]

The only exception to the exclusive use of school board–approved materials is special-education "individual educational plans." Guided by federal mandates, including strictly enforced time parameters, the IEP can utilize any content or materials deemed by experts to be necessary to meet the unique needs of each special-education student. Parents may even request modifications in the IEP.[30] Regular classroom teachers must be in full compliance with the IEPs when planning lessons for special-education students. School personnel must demonstrate that they know and understand the contents of the IEP and must be able to show how the proposed program and methodology will lead to attainment of the goals and objectives of the IEP.[31] Teachers must be in coordination with IEP guidelines at all times, or school districts may face court action as well as punitive damages.

Case in Point

LeVake v. Independent Sch. Dist. No. 656, 625 N.W.2d 502 (Minn. Ct.App. 2001)

A biology teacher is reassigned to another subject after he planned to teach criticisms of evolution rather than teach the prescribed biology curriculum. The teacher claimed that the reassignment violated his First Amendment rights to freedom of expression. Courts disagreed.

Talk It Over

A high school teacher who was attempting to teach world history invited representatives of several religious backgrounds into the classroom to explain their viewpoints. One such representative was a Wiccan priestess, schooled in witchcraft. Parents had not been informed of the content of the presentation prior to the speech. If you were a school administrator, what would your response to this idea have been?

Best-Practice Overview

Parents have a protected liberty under the PPRA (Protection of Pupils Rights Amendment), to review and inspect all instructional materials used by the school.[32] On the other hand, parents may not take their children out of specific courses, activities, or assignments unless specific provision is offered by the school board. Teachers should be aware of controversial subjects in the curriculum and seek administrator guidance as to how to proceed should a parent lodge a complaint. Forewarning parents that a lesson may include certain information is always a good idea. Providing an alternative assignment or activity allows parents to guide their children's education and defuses intense reactions in the community. Teachers must adhere to school-approved curriculum and use school-approved materials.

VOICES FROM THE FIELD—HOW SUCCESSFUL TEACHERS WORK WITH FAMILIES: GUIDELINES FOR SUCCESS

Sherrie Pardiek, EdD

As we entered the twenty-first century, family collaboration became a necessary and key component of our education system. National, state, and individual school districts expect teachers to have a plan to work with the families of students in their classrooms. Families can include parents, guardians, grandparents, extended family members, and siblings. The intent is to create student success through family and school partnerships for a community of learners.

Parents or primary caregivers are the first and most important teachers in a child's life. As educators, all of us are aware of family influences. Children will listen and learn from their parents or guardians and imitate learned information and behavior. Teachers have the daunting task of collaborating with a variety of family backgrounds, parenting styles, and family structures that exist within their classrooms.

Teachers will encounter a wide range of parenting styles and home environments: authoritarian and permissive homes, single-parent homes, homes with alternative lifestyles, at-risk homes, high- and low-income homes, and homes where English is a second language. Teachers must work with families through positive, respectful, and constant communication practices.

Respect for each and every family is of paramount importance. Many family members may have experienced social or academic failure in school. If they have retained negative attitudes toward the school environment, any attempts of communication may be dismissed as unimportant information. Teachers must provide opportunities for families to feel welcome and valued as important contributors in the student's learning experiences.

Communication methods can be incorporated through the use of newsletters, home visits, classroom responsibilities, email or phone calls, conferences, parent presentations, and teacher-family meetings. Classroom meetings can be social in nature and include snacks, meals, discussions of children's books, age-level issues, and learning activities that can be accomplished at home and school. Teachers should connect with families on a weekly basis. Informing the families about academic progress, school behavior, and current classroom learning activities is necessary for constant communication. Teacher and family meetings, whether they are social events or involve shared goal setting, should become a monthly activity. Then, families will feel valued and involved in their children's learning environment.

At the beginning of the year, teachers should have a meeting with the families in their classroom, including all members of each family, to outline goals and expectations for the school year. Goals can include specific responsibilities in the classroom, such as reading to students, helping with learning activities, field trips, and presentations of special talents, skills, or jobs. Behavioral expectations can also become a topic for discussion, as well as current social issues that face students of that grade level. Through constant communication and a variety of family activities, positive parent-teacher partnerships can flourish.

If teachers promote positive, constant, and respectful communications and classroom involvement with families, they will be able to provide the best learning environment for their students. As teacher and family partnerships are nourished in the classroom setting, the final outcome of these partnerships is student success within a community of learners.

CHAPTER 4

Drawing the Line with the School Administration

Key Concepts

Plenary power
Formal observations
Nepotism
School board policy
Background checks
Employment contract
Collective bargaining
Salary schedule
Insubordination
Immorality
Incompetence
Deficiency plan
Scope and sequence
Criterion testing
School improvement plan
Property right
Weingarten rights
Disaggregating data

This chapter will:

1. Identify job application criteria essential for teacher candidates.
2. Describe the elements of teaching contracts.
3. Explain the heavy regulation of the teaching profession as imposed by the courts.

(Continued)

4. Define incompetence, immorality, and insubordination as they apply to teaching contracts.
5. List the legal requirements for teaching evaluations for provisional contract teachers.

Teachers have a double duty to know and abide by the law—for themselves and for their students. School districts must be confident they have a capable and competent instructor in every classroom. Teachers are expected to know and be in compliance with (1) school board policy, (2) state school codes and statutes, and (3) current mandates in federal and judicial case law. Sounds intimidating, doesn't it? It is. Most school law cases each year deal with conflicts between school districts and teachers. Claiming ignorance of the law will not work on any level of legal responsibility. Simply pleading, "No one told me" is woefully insufficient when teachers are held responsible for actions they took in the classroom in their role as professional educators.

This chapter is divided to mirror the chronological flow of a teacher's career. First, the process of signing a professional contract is explained and directly connected to legal mandates and case law. Next, the first-year concerns of employment and professional behavior are covered. Finally, long-term career issues and decisions are touched upon. Each section offers several cases for further evaluation and discussion.

WHAT ARE THE LEGAL ASPECTS OF SEEKING EMPLOYMENT AS A TEACHER?

New graduates often are quite willing to do and say anything to get the job of their dreams. Thousands of hours and dollars (many in student loans) have been invested in career preparation, and highly motivated job applicants are willing to promise almost anything to get their foot in the door. Remember, school districts have certain rights vested in that job application. They include these:

- *Drug testing of applicants.* The Drug-free Schools and Communities Act Amendments of 1989 require all schools that receive federal assistance to establish programs covering both employees and students that are designed to prevent drug and alcohol abuse.[1]

- *Disclosure of relationships to other school district personnel or school board members.* Antinepotism laws often require that no school board member have relatives working in the school district. Additionally, many schools have policies that prohibit married teachers from being assigned to the same campus.[2]

- *Disclosure of applicant's private living arrangements.* The court test of "community morality standards" means that certain communities may not approve of unmarried partners living together, while other communities might. The job applicant is forewarned that school districts may in fact decide that the applicant's personal living arrangements are not considered appropriate for someone seeking a position that many see as a role model.[3] Applicants are reminded that local community standards for morality will guide and establish school district policies as law. When in Rome. . . .

- *Disclosure of prior criminal activity.* Most states require the fingerprinting of all student teachers and/or job applicants to ensure a safe school environment, free from teachers who have been convicted of felony crime. Additionally, online databases are currently being established to enable school administrators to screen teachers who have resigned while facing allegations of sexual misconduct. Many states have enacted legislation barring schools from entering into settlement agreements with teachers accused of sexual misconduct and also requiring school districts to disclose the reasons for any resulting resignations.[4] Job applicants may also have to certify that they have never been asked to resign from a teaching position. If they have, telling the truth may cost them the position. On the other hand, a teacher will certainly lose a job that was gained by pretense.[5]

- *Disclosure of prior disciplinary action by school administrators.* The Vermont Department of Education, among others, has established a Web site where it posts information on teacher disciplinary cases involving teachers. Such an initiative is not a new phenomenon, as information on nurses, accountants, and real estate agents is also available.[6]

- *Disclosure of health information.* All educators and student teachers must prove that they do not carry highly infectious airborne diseases such as tuberculosis.[7] Because federal and state courts require that schools maintain a "safe and healthy" environment for students, job applicants may need to disclose any health problems they have. They may also be required to take a physical stress test to demonstrate their ability to meet certain job requirements.[8]

- *Correct certification and educational preparation.* Many states expect applicants to disclose all professional preparation, such as graduate degrees, on an initial job application. When teachers fail to list graduate degrees in effort to hide additional college hours (and thereby lower their standing on the salary schedule) from potential employers, the employee will be dismissed, not for the additional course work but for making fraudulent statements on a job application.[9] Teachers must be able to prove that they have state certification for every subject they can teach under No Child Left Behind regulations that define "highly qualified teachers" status. Inflating the job application by listing areas where the applicant might qualify for certification will result in a dismissal should the state fail to certify the applicant in those subjects. In the same vein, false statements of citizenship will result in immediate dismissal.

Although job applicants have a constitutionally protected right to privacy, the governmental expectation that schools must provide a safe environment in the public interest overrides many individual rights.[10] The U.S Supreme court has concluded that the teaching profession is by its nature and out of necessity a "heavily regulated profession . . . thus reducing the expectation of privacy for the teachers." The U.S. Supreme Court has decided that teachers occupy "safety-sensitive" positions of public trust and therefore have a limited privacy right in their professional standing.[11]

Case in Point

Hoagland v. Mount Vernon School District, 95 Wn. 2d 424; 623 P. 2d 1156 (1981)

The school district determined that it had probable cause to dismiss a teacher who had been convicted of grand larceny by possession, because he had purchased a stolen motorcycle. The court found that the felony conviction was inherently harmful to the teacher-student relationship and therefore harmful to the school district. The teacher was not reinstated.

Talk It Over

A college student attending a Mardi Gras celebration was cited by local police for public urination—a misdemeanor act equal to a traffic ticket. When the student applied for a teaching certificate in his home state, he was denied certification because of the previous violation. The same act that was a misdemeanor in the first state was considered public indecency in his home state—a charge that would disqualify him from receiving state certification as a teacher. No appeal was possible; therefore, no teaching career.

Best-Practice Overview

All statements on a job application must be able to bear scrutiny by school district and law enforcement officials. A job application is not the place to write blatantly untrue or misleading statements regarding your professional preparation, personal or family relationships, and criminal or citizenship status. The job interview is tightly regulated by federal law as to the exact information that potential employers may or may not ask about, such as one's marital status or ethic background. On the other hand, untrue statements or misinformation supplied by the applicant will result in immediate dismissal once they are uncovered. The best advice to education majors is stay away from any and all criminal activity. The years of hard work they invested in professional preparation can be lost in a few minutes through actions resulting from a bad decision. Teachers are held to a higher standard by the courts because of the great trust and privilege they enjoy as teachers of the nation's youth.

WHAT RIGHTS DO TEACHERS HAVE WHEN SIGNING THE CONTRACT?

The first official act teachers perform as professionals is to sign a contract for their professional services with the school district or private school. That act alone begins a legal partnership. By law, the school district is granted certain rights and protections as the employer; the teacher is granted certain rights and protections as the employee.

To be valid, contracts must have five elements.

- First, the contact must be between competent parties. For example, a teacher must be eligible for or currently hold state certification.
- Second, there must be mutual assent. For example, the teacher must accept the contractual expectation of "duties as assigned by the board."
- Third, the contact must specify the amount of remuneration, based on the new teacher's place on the school district salary schedule as it appears in the collective-bargaining agreement.
- Fourth, it must indicate the duration of the contract, whether a specific school year or longer, as in the "continuing" contracts used in nontenure states.
- Fifth, the contract may not be illegal or in defiance of public policy. For example, the school board cannot contract for services that would stand in violation of state statute, such as hiring a teacher to teach a subject which the applicant does not hold state certification.

In summary, when teachers sign a contract, the school district must detail the faculty position for which the teacher has been hired, the salary step on which the teacher will be paid, the school year the contract will be in force, and any additional assignments the teacher will supervise. In many cases, the catchall phrase "duties as assigned" is used.[12] The contract is also premised upon the teacher's complete compliance with current school board policy. Finally, the contract ensures all parties equal standing in a court of law.

One thing to remember is that a signed contract does not ensure employment in a school district. The contract must be accepted by the board of education in an open vote of its members. Once the contract is accepted or "ratified" by the school board, it is in effect for the contract period. Power to employ or discharge teachers is vested exclusively in the school board and cannot be delegated to any other body or official, such as a superintendent.[13]

Why do the bulk of school law cases deal with conflicts between school districts and teachers? Dismissals and/or nonrenewals often occur in the course of a school year. Disagreements between faculty and administration may arise over the following:

- Teacher's incompetence.
- Teacher's immorality.
- Teacher's insubordination.
- Teacher's physical or mental disability.
- Teacher's unfitness or inadequate performance of duties.
- Reduction in force; no further need for teacher's services.
- Teacher's conviction of a felony or a crime involving moral turpitude.
- Teacher's failure to show normal improvement in professional training.

- Any cause that result in state revocation of the teacher's certificate or violations of state achievement testing security procedures.
- Teacher's nonperformance of duty.
- Teacher's failure to comply with reasonable orders by school administration.
- Teacher's violation of contract provisions or local rules or regulations.
- Teacher's persistent failure or refusal to maintain orderly discipline of students.
- "Good and just cause."

The first three terms are important and must be understood by every faculty member.

Insubordination includes a willful disregard of expressed or implied directions of the employer and a refusal to obey reasonable orders. Remember, the order must be legal and reasonable and must not infringe on the constitutional rights of the teachers or the students. Many cases of insubordination involve teachers who willfully do something they were told not to do. On the other hand, teachers also have been dismissed for not doing something, such as for being absent from an assigned duty station or failing to attend required meetings.[14] Taking sick leave under false pretenses also qualifies as insubordination. This might include, for example, attending a sporting event on a day the teacher had reported off as ill.

Incompetence refers to a lack of physical, intellectual, or moral ability, a general insufficiency or inadequacy or the want of legal qualification or fitness. Teachers who display a lack of subject-matter knowledge, cannot maintain classroom discipline, use unreasonable discipline, or willfully neglect their duty are deemed incompetent. Action such as showing an excessive number of films, leaving the classroom for extending times, failing to improve teaching strategies when given intervention, or failing to maintain order in the classroom open a teaching professional to charges of incompetence. One South Dakota court decided that incompetence must involve a pattern or course of conduct that reveals a habitual failure to perform work over an extended time period.[15]

Immorality involves behaving in a way that is contrary to good morals, inconsistent with the rules and principles of morality, or contrary to public welfare according to the standards of a given community.[16] Additionally, courts have added a "shocks the conscience" criterion for educational malpractice that includes immoral acts perpetrated against students.[17]

Historically, most American teachers have displayed high levels of professional competence, dependability, and moral character. Unfortunately, many do not. The three reasons for dismissal we have discussed—incompetence, insubordination, and immorality—are in every teacher's employment contract and may be reasons teachers are dismissed during the school year. Remember, the bearers of a current state teaching certificate are considered by the issuing state to have been shown to be professionally capable. The burden of proof otherwise is on the school board in a court of law.

As long as constitutionally protected rights (i.e., due process) and state law are followed by the school district, there is no legal requirement for school districts to issue continuing contracts, tenure, or provisional contracts to teachers they deem to have displayed behavior that is incompetent, immoral, or insubordinate.[18] Teachers who are past probationary status must be afforded due process. Many states even provide probationary teacher protection under state statutes if the teacher is dismissed during the school year. Nonetheless, school districts have been given considerable leeway to hire and fire as needed.[19] New teachers must be aware of their employment rights and read the employment contract carefully. Then teachers must fulfill all aspects of the employment contract.

In summary, employment contracts serve as the structure for teacher employment. Reading the contract very carefully will enlighten teachers as to the school board's expectation for their service. Teachers must be sure the information on the contract is accurate, reflects the verbal offer for a specific faculty position they were given during the interview, and has the correct salary schedule amount for the years of experience and education the teacher brings to the job.

Case in Point

Knox County Educ. Assn. v. Knox County Bd. of Educ., 953 S.W.2d 686 (Tenn. App. 1997)

A school district attempted to limit the number of years' experience it would recognize for teaching done out of their district. The district would not credit a teacher on the salary schedule for more than five years' out-of-district teaching. The court found that this school district could establish a salary schedule built on college preparation but could not nullify a teacher's work experience in out-of-district schools.

Talk It Over

A school district sends recruiters to a Spanish-speaking country to hire three teachers as staff in high school foreign language departments. The salary promised to the teachers is different from the salary schedule in place for district teachers. The school administration says the teachers do not have full American citizenship or state certification and places them on provisional pay status, outside the collective-bargaining agreement. Being on a provisional status also means the teachers do not receive full medical benefits or district sick or personal leave. Fair or not?

Best-Practice Overview

Job applicants should be very careful to read the contract they are signing. The school human resources department will gladly provide a copy of the salary schedule as affirmed in the collective-bargaining agreement with the teachers' association. *Teachers must ask for this information.* Such a request is not "beneath" a teaching professional. Rather, it is the natural result of their investment in college dollars spent. Teachers must find the precise pay level that they have earned in college hours and years of teaching experience and hold the school district to that amount.

Additionally, provisional teachers must remember the "ins" that can get them out—insubordination, immorality, and incompetence. Contracts are written for a purpose. In education, that purpose is to hire and retain educators who will act as professional representatives of the school board capably and competently.

ARE DRESS CODES FOR TEACHERS ENFORCED?

Many districts maintain dress codes for teachers. Specifically, school administrators expect a professional demeanor and a level of classroom decorum that are conducive to high student achievement. Without exception, the courts have supported districts embroiled in civil suits with teachers who did not want to adhere to dress codes. Issues raised in these cases have included the wearing of "long" hair, sideburns, or beards by men; a requirement that men wear neckties and/or jackets; and improper skirt length or immodest attire for women.

Teachers most often sue school boards for violating their First Amendment rights—that is, their right to freedom of speech—explaining that their appearance is a form of symbolic speech. Teachers quickly find themselves on the other side of *Tinker*, a precedent-setting court case that affirmed students' right to express themselves via their choice of clothing. Courts have not upheld such a finding for teachers. One court found, "As public servants in a special position of trust, teachers may properly be subjected to many restrictions in their professional lives which would be invalid if generally applied. In the view of the uniquely influential role of the public school teacher in the classroom, the board is justified in imposing this regulation."[20] Teachers are required to follow the district's dress code, even if the code has not been enforced on a regular basis. If the faculty objects to the dress code, the most effective manner of changing the dress code is to include the issue in collective-bargaining negotiations. Remember, the dress code is current school district policy. That fact alone carries the force of law.

Case in Point

East Hartford Education Association v. Board of Education of Town of East Hartford, 562 F.2d 856 (1977)

A teacher sued to be exempt from the school policy that all male teachers must wear a necktie in the classroom.

The teacher gave his reasons as follows:

- He wished to present himself to his students as a person who is not tied to "establishment conformity."
- He wished to symbolically indicate to his students his association with the ideas of the generation to which those students belong, including the rejection of many of the customs and values, and the social outlook, of the older generation.
- He felt that dress of this type (sans tie) enabled him to achieve closer rapport with his students and thus enhanced his ability to teach.

The court did not agree the teacher's rights had been violated in any way. The court expressed its reluctance to change policy: "We are expected here to balance the alleged interest in free expression against the goals of the school board. The school board's position must prevail."

Talk It Over

An elementary school allows its students to come to school wearing "flip-flops" or shower shoes during warm weather. A faculty member begins to wear the same foot attire during school hours while she is teaching. The school principal informs her that the dress code for teachers prohibits nonsoled footwear for faculty. The teacher is sent home, and docked pay, to replace the flip-flops with soled footwear, such as loafers. Several other teachers begin to show support for dress code violations by wearing sandals during the school day. Who is right?

Best-Practice Overview

Be sure to investigate the faculty dress code of any school district that extends the offer of a faculty position. Whether or not the code is currently being enforced, it has the force of law. Teachers may have options for appropriate dress depending on faculty assignments. Certain teachers, such as coaches, may be approved for "dress as appropriate for the setting" status. Otherwise, teachers must find their place in school board policy. As far as the court sees it, the only viable position for a faculty member is to be in complete compliance with all current school board polices and/or practices, including school district dress codes. Simply said—know school board policy and follow it.

WHY SHOULD TEACHERS BECOME MEMBERS OF PROFESSIONAL TEACHING ASSOCIATIONS?

Teaching is a profession. Across the nation, state statues regulate the profession of teaching, by controlling initial licensure, establishing recertification standards, providing regulation and review of ethical behavior, and establishing and accrediting teacher preparation programs. Historically, members of a profession have banded together for solidarity to further their mutual benefit, to further education in the field, to influence political action, and to regulate the profession. Teachers have in the past established many professional associations, both honorary and representational. For example, Phi Delta Kappa, an honorary educational association, is the nation's oldest professional educational association. PDK was founded more than 100 years ago for the mutual benefit of members in their quest to become more accomplished in educational pursuits. Phi Delta Kappa does not offer negotiation services to teachers. Two representational associations, National Education Association and the American Federation of Teachers, provide representation in collective-bargaining negotiations for their members.

Such teacher "unions" provide services for members, including these:

- *Liability insurance for professional practice.* Most unions offer liability insurance in the millions of dollars, as well as free access to attorneys who hold expertise in public school law.

- *Representation in grievance disputes with school administration.* In Weingarten rights, teachers may have union representatives (usually another teacher in the district) attend any conference with school administrators in which disciplinary action against the teacher may be discussed.

- *Political advocacy efforts at the state and federal levels.* Both large unions rally a cadre of professional and nonprofessional lobbyists to make their views known to state and federal lawmakers.

- *Professional growth opportunities.* Many states require ongoing professional development for teachers as a basis for certificate renewal. Unions offer workshops and courses designed to meet specific state standards.

School districts may not require teachers to join a professional association. On the other hand, teachers in a school district may choose a primary association to do all their collective bargaining. In that case, teachers who are not union members must pay their "fair share" of union costs, such as collective-bargaining costs and agency expenses.[21] Further, in states where unions are not recognized as collective-bargaining agents, specific procedures are in place to ensure that teachers may talk about union activity during school hours and use the inter-school post to share printed union materials—without fear of reprisal.[22]

Case in Point

Nashua Teacher Union v. Nashua School Dist., 707 A2d 448 (N.H. 1998)

In a school that was a so-called fair-share shop, a few teachers did not want to pay their "agency fees" or the costs associated with collective bargaining for the entire district. Even though the agency fees were lower than regular membership fees for union members, the teachers took the school district to court for automatically deducting the fees from their paychecks. The court rejected the teachers' claim and held that the compulsory fees were lawful, as was the practice of automatic deduction from the paycheck.

Talk It Over

A school principal requests that a teacher come to her office in reference to a parent complaint about his teaching methods. When the teacher appears, he is accompanied by the union representative, another teacher on faculty in the school. The principal quips, "If you have nothing to hide, you should not need your union rep with you." What would the courts say about his remark?

Best-Practice Overview

Although no one can enforce membership in professional unions, many teachers join for wise reasons. They include the following:

1. *Liability insurance.* Teachers have the responsibility for students in many dangerous situations, such as field trips, sports practices, and recess play. Should a student be injured, the association will step in to legally support the teacher with funding and provide a knowledgeable legal representative who is well versed in school law.
2. *Mentoring opportunities for new teachers.* Association members are often willing to give of their own time to help a new teacher become established in the school and district.
3. *Professional development.* Teacher associations often fund teacher-training workshops and seminars designed to meet the recertification needs of the teachers in their state.
4. *Faculty advocates in disputes with school administration or parents.* Having another teacher with you as moral support helps in times of intense pressure resulting from petty complaints.

All of these reasons provide the impetus for membership. Nonetheless, each teacher must make her own personal decision; no administrator may pressure or coerce the faculty member in any way. Remember, fair-share fees may be deducted from your pay if the district has a single association that negotiates collective-bargaining agreements for all teachers in the district, since the association bargains for pay and benefits for all teachers, not just those who are members. All teachers benefit from the negotiations. If you are a member, you will have direct input and a vote in the collecting-bargaining agreement. That alone is worth the membership dues.

FIRST-YEAR ISSUES: HOW WILL SCHOOL ADMINISTRATORS EVALUATE TEACHERS?

The first year of employment is a busy and stressful time for novice teachers. Often, simply meeting the demands of school schedules, extracurricular activities, parent conferences, and grading requirements involving mountains of papers is overwhelming. Nonetheless, teachers do survive, and then they turn to help other first-year teachers do the same. Many legal issues arise during those first years, which often go unspoken during college preparation. They include assignment to extra duties, academic freedom, direct observation of classroom teaching by administrators, deficiency plans, committee work, standardized testing security, the handling of school funds, and media involvement. One can only imagine the yeoman effort needed to complete the first year successfully.

New teachers may be in the classroom barely a few weeks when the first observation is scheduled by administrators. Intimidating and uncomfortable, the first direct observation by a direct supervisor isn't the same as observations conducted during student teaching. Now, the focus has changed from supporting growth of the teacher to assessment for employment purposes. That shift alone gives cause for increased concern and implies that this observation is more than simply something to endure. Observations conducted by school administrators will be used for determining future employment and will find their way into the next level of employment, whatever that may be. Certainly, then, the importance of the first year's observation and assessment record cannot be understated.

Evaluations by school administrators are under the complete control of the school board, with input from collective-bargaining agreements. Remember, the courts have granted the school board wide license to hire and fire as they wish, within the parameters of state law and constitutional mandates.[23] According to the U.S. Supreme Court, provisional teachers have no right to expect a clearly stated reason for the nonrenewal of their contract at the end of their contract year.[24] Frustrating? Yes! Even principals have little or no job security and face the possibility of nonrenewal of their administrative contracts. Demonstrating a high level of professionalism during the first year is essential.

Classroom observations may take many forms. They include:

1. *Informal observation.* Supervisors may simply view the teacher's interaction with student and other faculty in school hallways, after school activities, and during lunch. Administrators may conduct "walk-through" visits to the classroom and stay a few moments at the longest.
2. *Formal observation.* A time is set for the principal or supervisor to visit the class.

   a. Supervisors may videotape the teaching performance.[25]
   b. Supervisors may sit in on classes and take notes during the lesson.
   c. Supervisors may script the lesson (write every word said by teacher and students).
   d. Supervisors may use an observation format devised by the district or state. Usually these instruments utilize a list of descriptors such as, "Involves all students in the lesson."
   e. Supervisors may use a preconference with the teacher to set specific set of goals for the lesson and then check to see if those goals were met.

Finally, direct observations may be scheduled or unscheduled. That is, the supervisor may set a time in advance of the observation, ask the teacher which lesson time would be best for them, or simply walk into the classroom and sit down. It is not uncommon, for school principals to do several "walk-through" visits prior to the first formal observation.

Teachers should provide their administrator with important information prior to the formal observation. This information would include the following:

- The names and seating placements of students in the class who have IEPs from special-education placement.
- The names and seating placements of students who may become uncooperative during class.
- A complete lesson plan of the instruction, including the previous day's lesson goals and the instructional lesson to follow.
- A seating chart of the class.
- A statement of the teacher's learning and assessment goals for the lesson.
- Correlation of the lesson objectives with state learning goals.
- A copy of all student materials to be used in the lesson.
- A copy of the classroom rules.

When administrators have ample materials from which to give high-quality assessments, the teacher has the opportunity to shine.

After the observation, supervisors should, but are not required by law to, share their observation materials with the teacher. If specific weaknesses are identified, the school administrator should provide those in writing to the teacher, as well as a plan for remediation. Often titled "deficiency plans," the document should offer a timeline for completion and refer the teacher to specific resources for professional growth. Meeting the deficiency-plan goals is critical if the teacher is to remain in the school district's employ. This is not a time for obstinacy; rather, it is a time for cooperation and a willingness to comply with suggestions by your employers. On the other hand, many school supervisors are extremely complimentary about the teacher they observed, and yet the teacher receives news of nonrenewal in the spring. No guarantees are offered to teachers who lack continuing contracts or tenure. On the other hand, should school districts dismiss the teacher *during the life of the contract*, all constitutional rights of due process must be afforded to the teacher; nonrenewal at the end of the contact time period carries no such constitutional protections.

Case in Point

Evens v. Superior Court of Los Angeles County, 77 Cal. App. 4th 320 (1999)

Students videotaped a teacher conducting a math class as a means of proving her incompetence in disciplinary control to the school board. The teacher and the local association sued to stop the tape from being used by school administration for evaluation purposes. The court held that the tape could be used for evaluation purposes, as the state statutes did not prohibit the taping of the teacher's lesson. Also, the court reasoned that the tape was done in a public classroom, where the teacher had no expectation of privacy.

Talk It Over

A teacher was told to correct his students' wild and inappropriate behavior in class. He was directed by his principal to "handle it any way you know how." The teacher used a two-foot cattle prod to administer an electronic shock to students who failed to follow his directions. The teacher was dismissed. The court reinstated him, because no permanent injury was done to the student.[26] What do you think?

Best-Practice Overview

Observations of teaching can take many forms; most all are outlined in the collective-bargaining agreement in the school district. The teacher has no right to bar any supervisory personnel from the classroom at any time. As a result, observations may take place at any time—scheduled or unscheduled. Teachers should be well prepared for every formal conference and not attempt to "fly by the seat of their pants." High levels of preparation provide a high level of self-confidence. It is impossible to undo the bad impression made during a poor observation.

Observation notes and evaluation materials are the property of the school district, but a summary of the observation must be provided to the teacher in a timely manner. Deficiency plans must be specific and identify acceptable timelines and resources available from the district. In many states, teachers who face nonrenewal for any reason—or no reason—must be given written notice by early spring, usually by March 1 or April 1. If no written notice is given, the teacher must be rehired for the following academic year. The teacher association in the school district will provide teachers written notice of all legal guidelines, timelines, and school board responsibilities.

Simply said, provisional teachers have no legal right to continued employment, regardless of their proficiency in the classroom. Continuing-contract and tenured teachers have a constitutional protection to a property right of continued employment. All teachers are guaranteed due process under the Constitution if they are dismissed during the life of the contract—unless the dismissal is as a direct result of insubordination, immorality, or incompetence.

MUST TEACHERS USE ONLY APPROVED CURRICULUM ADOPTION AND CLASSROOM MATERIALS?

Teachers fresh from college graduation dream of the day they can craft their own classroom lessons—teaching their favorite subjects. In fact, studies show, teachers tend to select instructional materials on the basis of their own interests.[27] Unfortunately, the reality of state standardized testing, No Child Left Behind mandates, special-education IEPs, and school-board-approved textbooks begins to curb the teacher's ability to arbitrarily select curriculum materials. Gone are the days when teachers could spend three weeks exploring butterflies in science and poetry. If that subject is not in the scope and sequence of school-board-approved skills for that grade level, the subject is disapproved for introduction to students. A cold fact—but true.

Further, new teachers are often assigned to sit on curriculum committees. Such committees review all state-approved textbooks and make recommendations to school administrators about which text is best for the district. Although many teachers feel this is a waste of their time, they are wrong. Simply by participating in textbook review, the teacher has become part of the advisory process that school boards rely upon to select appropriate materials representative of the community and students. By requiring teachers to sit on such committees, the school board has solicited expert opinion as well as community input before it establishes a course of study and purchases the materials.

When teachers have overstepped their bounds by teaching curriculum that is not board-approved for their grade levels, selecting nonapproved materials, or introducing concepts considered against community standard, they have been dismissed. Courts have also declared that specific methods of teaching, if in opposition to school board standards, are not acceptable. For example, a group of social studies teaches sued their district for the right to "team teach" small-group, independent, and discovery techniques to their classes, in a course far from the norm. The court responded: "Course content (including methods used) is manifestly a matter within the board's discretion."[28]

No matter which way the point is made, curriculum is the domain of the school board without exception. Teaches may have input as to age-appropriate classroom subjects and materials only as they accept leadership in curriculum committees.

Note: Teachers have been officially admonished after buying gifts (books, DVDs, or CDs) for students if those gifts carry information outside the prescribed curriculum.[29] Buyer, beware!

Case in Point

Cowan v. Strafford R-VI School District, 140 F3d 1153 (1998)

A second-grade teacher sent her students home at the end of the school year with a rock and the following note taped to it:

Dear Second Grader:

You have completed second grade. Because you have worked so hard, you deserve something special and unique just like you! That something special is your very own magic rock. The magic rock you have will always let you know that you can do anything that you set you mind to. To make your rock work, close your eyes, rub it, and say to yourself three times, "I am a special and terrific person, with talents of my own!" Before you put your rock away, think of three good things about yourself. After you have put your rock away, you will know the magic worked.

HAVE FUN IN THIRD GRADE!!!!!

Parents reacted to this as "New Age" philosophy. The teacher attributed her subsequent dismissal to this note. Although the court did not agree that the teacher should be reinstated (she was on a provisional contract), it did award her two years' pay.

Talk It Over

An educator at a middle school teaches the period of the American Civil War. During the war unit, he has students draw self-portraits to put on large posters that advertise a bounty paid for the return of runaway slaves. The posters are hung in the main school hallway. Then, in a classroom reenactment, students are tied hand and foot by rubber bands and left on the floor to simulate the cramped conditions of those imprisoned in the holds of slave ships. As a parent, what would you say about the teaching strategies?

Best-Practice Overview

Academic freedom is not constitutionally protected for elementary and secondary teachers. They are considered dispensers of knowledge—not researchers, as in college and university settings.
Teachers must:

1. Be aware of the curriculum scope and sequence approved by the school board for the assigned grade level.
2. Keep all teaching based solely upon board-approved materials.
3. Have new or unusual teaching methods approved by the school administrator before the instruction is implemented.
4. Be concerned about and sensitive to community norms and parental expectations.
5. Base all instruction on textbooks approved by the board, even if those books include only a shortened version of the materials you want to teach.
6. Have all supplemental material approved by your school administrator.
7. Be sure all lessons have direct connections to state learning goals.

Unique to the profession of teaching is the assumption that a novice teacher can do the work of a veteran teacher. In many school districts, first-year teachers are assigned to teach class loads, subjects, and schedules like those of experienced teachers in the same school. The classroom seems to be a "kingdom of the door." That is, once the classroom door is closed, every teacher must perform the job, regardless of years of experience or depth of professional preparation. Unfortunately, the sense of isolation—no one can see what I do here—is a false impression. Teachers are not authorities unto themselves. They are employed under legal authority. Teachers, regardless of their experience level, are held responsible for meeting all school board standards for curriculum and instruction. The classroom door is very transparent, indeed.

CAREER CONCERNS: HOW SHOULD SCHOOL FUNDS AND SCHOOL PROPERTY BE HANDLED?

All teachers handle money, often with little or no understanding of school accounting procedures. Teachers assigned to extracurricular activities quickly find themselves in fundraising endeavors. Teachers in the elementary school often hand out advertising from book companies eager to sell paperback books to parents of grade-school students. Teachers purchase items from their own students as a show of support for a worthy cause. Teachers request reimbursement for items purchased for the classroom or for student organization activities. Teachers give lunch money to students who otherwise would be hungry. School districts have specific procedures for accounting for all funds taken in or spent by faculty. These procedures are crafted to ensure that the school district can withstand the scrutiny of an external auditing review. Allowing teachers to place cash in their desks, their personal accounts, or their homes is a bad idea. When teachers deposit "book" money in their accounts, deposit parent's personal checks for materials or parties in their personal accounts, or hold onto money in cash form, the documents required for a clean financial review are never generated. That opens the door for accusations of wrongdoing on the teacher's or the school administrator's part. School accounting procedures are unique to the school and the district. It is the teacher's responsibility to know and be in complete compliance with all school board policies regarding money. *No* exceptions will be allowed by external reviewers. Violators will be subject to a criminal charge of theft. Teacher associations will not provide funding or legal representation in the event of a criminal charge against the teacher.

Additionally, teachers deal with thousands of dollars in school equipment every day. Missing or damaged equipment can and will be the responsibility of the person who accepted responsibility for that item. In many schools across the nation, teachers are held financially responsible for lost student textbooks at the end of the year, because the teacher must sign for the books at the start of the year. Teachers do not have the right to send equipment home with their students or to lend materials or equipment to parents.

For example, allowing students to take home library dictionaries, atlases, or encyclopedias sets the teacher in defiance of school board policy and at risk of having to replace the item at the current replacement cost—which may be quite high. Finally, taking home equipment such as computers, sewing machines, or typewriters because they are going to be thrown away or not utilized over the summer is shortsighted. Unless the school administrator is willing to put the "gift" in writing, wait to buy it at a school district auction. Fast deals that result from slow ethical thinking can result in the revocation of a state teaching certificate, which is worth far more than an outdated piece of technology or a few weeks' use of school property in the summer.

Case in Point

Mitchell v. Board of Education of Fayette County, Fed. App. 0225P 6th Cir. (2004)

A school custodian was dismissed after allegations that he helped another custodian take a sewing machine, several ladders, lumber, and folding chairs from a school in which he was employed. The school district received the allegation from an unnamed source. No criminal action was ever taken, but the custodian was fired.

Talk It Over

A teacher who serves as a cheerleading sponsor allows current students to take home pompoms that were used several years ago. The students gladly take the old equipment. Parents of past squad members complain because they raised the funds for the purchase of that equipment. The understanding at that time was that the equipment would be "handed down" to the middle school students when the high school was finished using the materials. Current replacement price for the equipment is more than $500. The teacher decides to pay the replacement costs rather than answer grand theft charges. Fair or not?

Best-Practice Overview

Most teachers do not go into the education profession for money. Unfortunately, they often transfer this disregard for money to their school funding activities. Every dollar spent for students or gathered from students must be documented and accounted for by a paper receipt. Teachers who give money to the school administrator to be locked in the school vault must get a receipt simply to show that deposit was made. That is the only fail-safe process to ensure that the money will be there when the teacher returns for it a few days or months in the future. All book orders, uniform money, fundraising monies, or gifts from parents or other community members must be deposited with the *full knowledge of the local school administrator,* and the teacher should insist on a dated receipt with a signature. A teacher writes the receipt, a secretary signs and dates it. School accounting procedures are not negotiable. The school administrator must be able to show where every penny came from and where it was spent.

The combination of kids and money poses a risk! No money can be left in the teacher's desk. Cash poses a temptation for any student who may want the money for a trip to the local carnival. No money should ever be given directly to students—not even for lunch. The teacher should accompany the student to the cafeteria and pay the lunch personnel directly for any food. If the teacher fails to accompany the student or to have a responsible adult pay for the food, the student may have grounds to say the money was tendered for immoral reasons (this has happened)! If the teacher purchases an item from a student who may be involved in fundraising for a nonschool activity, such as scouting, the teacher should not pay in cash. Offer a personal check and note why the money was given. Do not make the check out to the student or to the parents; make it out to the organization sponsoring the sale. Be prepared to never see the materials. That has happened, as well!

Do not offer school property to parents for their use or take any school inventoried materials out of the school for any reason. Do not help another teacher to do so. Extracurricular activity teachers often share school materials such as music sheets, drama costumes, sports materials, books, and equipment, as well as keys to school facilities. Never do this! All school materials must remain for the use designated by the school board. Do not open the school facility to community members or parents without clear, written approval from school administrators. Vandalism and injury can result when the school is opened at nonapproved times. The teachers who hold the keys are held personally responsible for liability damages stemming from unauthorized actions.[30] Be sure all school materials have been returned and are secure before leaving the campus or activity. Be sure any lost keys are quickly reported to the school office; the entire facility may have to be re-keyed as a result of the loss.

Finally, if the teacher receives money to purchase materials for their classroom, the teacher must comply with all accounting procedures and clearly mark the materials as school-district property. Any materials purchased with school funds must be left with the front office before the teacher changes to another campus. Just because the materials were purchased for one teacher's unique interests, that doesn't mean the materials belong to the teacher if they were purchased with school funds. Simply said, be honest and forthright in all monetary dealing with the school board, school administrators, and other teachers—no exceptions. The school may feel like home, but it is not. It belongs to the school board for that school district and must be treated with care and respect. Why lose a job over a few dollars? Remember, many states now require school districts to report any teacher who was asked to resign for any reason.

WHAT ARE THE RULES FOR STANDARDIZED TESTING COMPLIANCE?

The state has established uniform testing for grades three, five, eight, and eleven to monitor the acquisition of basic skills by students statewide. Each district school board is also required to establish pupil progression plans to insure that students are not promoted without consideration of each student's mastery of basic skills.

Debra P. v. Turlington, 564 F. Supp 177 aff'd 730 F2d. (1984)

The courts have consistently held that the power over education is an essential activity of state sovereignty. All states have established systems of public schools that operate as administrative arms of state government. State legislatures have plenary power over the schools—that is, power that is complete, absolute, and unqualified.[31] Early in our nation's history, the power of the state legislature to overrule local governance set the stage for state control of the school finance, administration, and curriculum. In the past 100 years, states have established standards for teacher certification and the testing of student achievement.

When states have allowed local districts to use whatever student achievement testing they choose, the districts have selected skill (criterion) testing or ability testing as the local school board deemed fit. (Ability testing is standardized testing that reports the level [grade or age] at which the individual student is learning. Criterion tests such as the Iowa Test of Basic Skills report what skills and concepts the student has mastered.) Ability tests such as IQ tests are based on the comparison of students with others in their age group. Some school districts opted to construct their own tests and administered those yearly to facilitate promotion and retention decisions.

Although local school board control of student testing was allowed by many states, the move in the 1970s to increased federal interventions in local schools brought an increased use of nationally available standardized test instruments by local school districts. Such tests allowed districts to compare themselves with school districts across the United States. Accountability standards from the 1980s, pushed by both federal and states legislatures, widened the use of state-developed or nationally known standardized tests. Currently, No Child Left Behind, the federal mandate for all schools that receive governmental monetary support, mandates that all states have a complete cohort of statistically reliable, norm-referenced tests to provide the public with testing results per school—and that information must be readily available to the public via the state board of education Web site and must be published in local newspapers by October of each academic year. An interesting aspect of NCLB allows students in failing schools to transfer within their districts to schools with higher levels of student achievements, as reported by standardized testing. This new flexibility has only increased the accountability for all schools and school districts.[32] No observer of American schools can fail to note the importance of standardized testing to the financial health and community confidence level of local schools.

Teachers are the lifeblood of standardized testing. Teachers perform many jobs that are essential for the successful and accurate completion of standardized testing. They participate in these areas:

- *Construction of the tests.* Many states employ teacher representatives from across the state to construct sample questions, to evaluate current questions for demographic fairness and content validity, and to help correlate questions with district curriculum.

- *Student preparation for the tests.* All instruction in the classroom rests on the shoulders of the teachers. Not only is the test content the single focus of instruction, but test-wariness is also taught. This is the practice of teaching students how to take a test so as to increase the likelihood they will not be confused by test procedures or appearance.

- *Maintenance of test security.* Teachers must sign a statement that they will comply with all state-approved procedures for handling, storing, and administering test materials. Standardized testing becomes inaccurate and ineffective when teachers fail to protocols for test handling and administration.

- *Interpretation of testing results in the local school.* Many states require individual schools to evaluate all test results and to formulate immediate and long-term goals to improve the test scores for the next academic year. Often called "School Improvement Plans" or "Student Achievement Plans," they require the faculty to evaluate, formulate, and implement plans for high student achievement (as reported by standardized test achievement). These formal plans are submitted to both local school district administration and the state board of education. The plan becomes the action target for the next year's round of standardized testing results. Testing results should be broken down into age, gender, and racial groupings. This process is called disaggregating data. It is used to compare one group against another and to detect groups that are underserved or that fail to progress. (Disaggregating data is at the heart of our democracy. Remember the phrase "For all" in our pledge to the flag. Education must be "for all," not just for the frontrunners and high achievers).

Standardized testing impacts teachers in every aspect of their teaching, but one single issue stands out as primary. That is test security.

"I am discussing with the State Board of Education that the school district be assessed a sum of money as a consequence of the actions of their employees," former Illinois state superintendent Dr. Robert Schiller commented as he responded to the investigation of a school faculty member and an administrator who allegedly compromised state test procedures.[33] With those words, released on the Illinois State Board of Education Web site on August 13, 2003, Dr. Schiller got to the heart of standardized testing. This policy is mandated by law and enforced by the state board of education.[34]

Standardized testing is essential for school districts to provide accountability for student achievement to the general public. School boards expect teachers to be in strict compliance with requirements for the storage, administration, and handling of standardized tests. When violation occurs, everyone loses. Should infractions of test security or administration occur, the school district stands to lose federal and state funding, and the teacher and/or school administrator stands to lose employment and their state certificate. Many states have suspended teachers who have posted sample questions on the school Web site.[35] Whether or not teachers agree with the use of testing to show student achievement, the fact remains—tests are used for that purpose, and the professional educator will comply with all legal mandates.

Case in Point

Rene v. Reed, 751 N.E.2d 736 (Ind. Ct.App. 2001)

The Indiana Court of Appeals found that special-education students were not denied their rights under IDEA. The students claimed that they had not received testing modifications as given under their IEPs. Although the school had supplied certain testing modifications, such as questions in Braille, special lighting, sign-language responses, special furniture, and small-group testing, it had denied accommodations in the form of having the questions read aloud and unlimited testing time. The court also upheld the school district's withholding of graduation diplomas from students who had not passed the state standardized test.

Talk It Over

A high school English teacher was observed walking abound the room, stopping at each student's desk to point out one correct answer to each student during state testing. She had promised a "freebie" to each student in her class if the students tried their best on the exam. What do you think? How much damage can one free answer do to a student's score? How much damage can one free answer do to the teacher's career?

Best-Practice Overview

The best and safest pathway for all teachers to tread during state testing is to do exactly what the standardized testing procedure manual says to do and nothing more. No violations will be acceptable. You cannot do students favors by helping them across the finish line. The "help" you give them may in fact invalidate all of the school's testing results and bring state fines upon the entire school district. Get on the school improvement committee and make your thoughts known. Help students prepare for state testing by teaching the materials as approved by the school board.

Test security requires:

- Signing a statement of intent before you pick up your tests.
- Storing the tests in a locked cabinet.

- Preparing students and parents regarding good health practices prior to testing.
- Never making a copy of any page of the test instrument.
- Not reading questions for students.
- Not explaining tests question charts or tables for students.
- Not allowing students to exit the testing room during the test. (Should students need to leave, the test they have been working on must be closed at the last question they completed, and the test monitor must not allow the student to finish when they return.)
- Being precise in all time limits for tests, down to the second.
- Being sure the tests are locked and secure between administrations.
- Being watchful during the test period, and walking around the classroom during the testing.
- Providing correct writing instruments for students who fail to bring their own.
- Not encouraging students who finish early to read magazines or other free reading materials (many students will hurry though testing to get to fun reading).
- Returning tests on time and putting them into the correct person's care.
- Reporting any faculty violations as soon as you witness them (do not ignore a situation that can only become worse).

Tests are an inevitable part of public education. Learn to administer standardized tests as a professional educator. Best advice to new teachers? Get involved with the school improvement committee and make your voice count in the overall goals of the school. Utilize standardized testing as it was intended to be used, as one measure of student achievement.

WHAT ARE EMPLOYMENT DISCIPLINARY CONFERENCES AND GRIEVANCE PROCEDURES?

As a provisionary or tenured teacher, the only safeguard one has against unfair treatment by school administration is the union-negotiated collective-bargaining agreement. Several pathways are available for the teacher. Each one has very specific procedures, and only an attorney can identify the most promising for the teacher to select. If the teacher is a union member, school attorneys are available at no cost. If the teacher has not joined any association, they must bear the cost of legal advice. Of course, if the teacher chooses not to grieve or enact a lawsuit, that is the teacher's personal decision. Many teachers choose to meet unfair treatment with stalwart silence.

If, in fact, they do decide to use the process designed for such situations, the timelines built into the school board policy are critical. For example, some time frames are expressed in "business days," some in "calendar days," and some in "school days." How will the teacher know what the board has cited as a "day"? Only a union representative or school law attorney will be able to help the teacher understand the levels of deadlines and progress toward a resolution of the grievance or due process violation.

Key ideas for completing a grievance include the following:

- The teacher must understand school board policy as it applies to the specific situation and must follow all steps for resolution of the problem. Have the latest iteration of the policy in writing.
- Timelines must be met or the teacher forfeits the right to any appeal.
- All meetings must include the teacher, as well as any representative the teacher wishes to include. Include the building association representatives as early as possible in the grievance process.
- There must be a written record of the actions taken and testimony presented as evidence at all meetings (no secret meetings or secret testimony can be used in any decision regarding employment).
- Because the school board serves as an arm of the state government, teachers have the right to appeal any school board decision to governmental agencies such as the Equal Employment Opportunity Commission, the Office of Civil Rights, Workman's Compensation Boards, and/or the state Fair Practices Commission.[36] Your attorney or union representative will know which is best to hear your complaint. *Ask them! Do not be shy!*
- The teacher may have governmental protection such as Title IX retaliation immunity or whistleblower immunity if the adverse employment action is in retaliation for the teacher's reporting violations of federal mandates.
- Civil court action must involve some type of contract violation or constitutional protections issue.

Imagine the following situations:

1. A teacher is assigned to coach a girl's basketball team as part of her faculty position. Prior to the start of the season, the coaching position offer is withdrawn, as well as the expected stipend. If the employment contract has identified the basketball position as part of the teacher's responsibility, the option exists for utilizing the district grievance procedure. On the other hand, if the contract contains no mention of the sports position, no violation of the employment contract has occurred. Next time, get it in writing.
2. If the teacher is dismissed in the middle of the contract, the opportunity exists for a civil law suit for violation of due process. Begin a civil suit for loss of property rights. A property right is the right to specific property, whether it is personal or real property, tangible or intangible. Teachers have a property right to continued employment.
3. Parents complain about the end-of-year gifts a teacher gives to his students. The gifts are representations of a popular child's literature hero who uses witchcraft. The school district may discipline that teacher if the school-board-approved curriculum has eliminated all stories about witchcraft from the classroom. Know your curriculum, and stay within it. No appeal is possible here. The school board rules. Accept the correction. Apologize. Don't make that mistake again.

4. A teacher complains that boys' and girls' sports facilities are unequal. The teacher is removed from the coaching staff. If the allegations are true and can be shown to be true, this is a Title IX violation. The teacher's job cannot be taken away, because there are federally mandated whistleblower protections.[37]
5. A teacher suffers sexual harassment by a student. The teacher is ignored by school administrators when she reports the harassment. This is another Title IX violation. The Office of Civil Rights will intervene.[38]

Remember, a teacher must give the school district the first opportunity to correct the troublesome situation. All governmental agencies will expect that they are *not the first step* in a grievance procedure. Further, teachers are encouraged to be aware of any school administrative response to the filing of a grievance. Employment settings may not be made unpleasant to the point that a "hostile environment" or a "constructive discharge" is created. (If the employer has made the working condition so intolerable that a reasonable employee would be forced to leave, this is termed a "constructive discharge.")[39] A hostile environment has been created when the harassing behavior of anyone in the workplace causes the workplace to become hostile, intimidating, or offensive.[40]A change in employment may be part of a settlement agreement. Teachers need to be sure they have followed the collective-bargaining agreement timelines and criteria to avoid forced or involuntary transfer.

Remember, each situation is different, and generalizations are not helpful in selecting the right path for a teacher's response. Only the union representative or an attorney can give competent advice in each situation.

Please note that I do not purport to give any blanket advice in any of the scenarios I have described. The only recommendation that will benefit all teachers is to be an active advocate in their own best interest regarding grievance situations with the school board. Be informed about school board policy. That policy creates the rules for the district grievance procedure. The court will expect the school board to follow its own rules to the detail—both the spirit and the letter of the policy are important.

Finally, resignations are not in the best interest of the teacher. Current policy in most states requires school districts to identify any teacher who resigns at the request of the school board. The "pass the trash" practices of many years ago are being changed by state law. In years past, teachers of questionable moral and ethical standing were allowed to leave the district quietly and to find further employment in an unsuspecting school district. That practice is being halted. Job applications in law-savvy districts will include the question "Have you ever resigned from a teaching position?" A positive response to this question is the signal that there are additional issues with this teacher's employment fitness. Misrepresentation of any information on the job application is grounds for immediate dismissal.[41] Unless teachers want to try another line of work, a resignation is not the best way to respond to a grievance with school administrators.

Case in Point

Princeton City School Dist Bd. of Educ. v. Princeton Assn. of Classroom Educators, OEA/NEA, 731 N.E.2d 186 (Ohio App. 1st Dist. 1999)

A student posing for a class picture "mooned" the camera. The teacher in charge of the group failed to notify the school guidance counselor of the student's behavior until several weeks after the picture was developed. At that time, the student was expelled, and the teacher was suspended for taking such an inappropriate picture and for failing to report serious student misconduct. The teacher's collective-bargaining association filed a grievance and obtained a favorable ruling on the arbitrator's finding that the school board did not have good and just cause for disciplining the teacher.

Talk It Over

A first-year teacher elementary teacher continues to be the target of sexually charged jokes and comments from the female principal during faculty meetings. The teacher has ignored the behavior for months, because he does want to appear uncooperative and wishes not to insult the women on staff or in the administration at the school. What should he do?

Best-Practice Overview

Teachers must be aware that they have specific employment rights as granted by employment contract, collective-bargaining agreements, and school policy (both current practice and board approved). When disputes arise, all three of these may provide opportunities for resolution of the problem. Teachers who defer their rights to a positive, professional working environment give up their most important asset as educators.

Teachers must remember the following options when disagreements arise:

- Don't let little issues escalate until emotions are high.
- Try to resolve the dispute in the most immediate manner. Talk it over with your union representative and school administration. Be workable, and strive for a positive resolution.
- Do not be afraid to file a grievance when the situation is intolerable and all attempts to discuss the situation have failed.
- Follow all procedures as outlined in school board grievance policy.
- Our society is based on rule of law. Use it!
- Be patient, large organizations like school districts are very resistant to change.

GUIDELINES FOR SUCCESS—HOW SUCCESSFUL
TEACHERS WORK WITH THEIR COLLEAGUES
Dr. Shari Britner

Colleagues can be your most important source of mentoring and support; however, they also occasionally can present challenges to your professionalism and integrity. Your goal in your first few years of teaching should be to learn to maximize the former and safely negotiate the latter.

There are a variety of individuals who may be considered your colleagues, including district and building-level administrators, union and professional-organization personnel, teachers in your school, teachers in other schools, and paraprofessionals and staff in your school. The wide range of individuals who are your colleagues increases the sources of knowledge and support available to you. Don't fall into the trap of viewing administrators as the enemy or secretarial and cafeteria staff as being beneath your level. Just as it takes a village to raise a child, it takes professionals at all levels to create a smoothly functioning school. The more alliances you build at each of these levels, the greater the contribution you will be able to make.

If you are lucky, your school will assign you a mentor, a more experienced teacher whose job it will be to show you the ropes on your new job and to support you as you deal with the triumphs and challenges faced by all new teachers. Probably you also will develop informal mentoring relationships with other teachers in your school, as most teachers are eager to help new teachers. Don't hesitate to ask for help or advice from the teacher next door or the teacher at lunch who seems friendly. You may find that you make a stronger connection informally than with your official mentor, or you may simply create an additional relationship that adds to your support network.

Here are some suggestions from my own experience as a teacher, from my experience supervising student teachers, and from beginning teachers:

1. Don't be afraid to ask for help. There are really two aspects to this recommendation. The first is to accept that you will need help in the beginning; other teachers and administrators expect you to need help, and it is part of their job to help new teachers succeed. The second part is to speak up and ask for what you need. Don't assume that it is obvious; if you don't ask, your colleagues may assume that you don't need or want their assistance.
2. Make sure right from the start that you are making a contribution in collaborative relationships. Do your part when working with your team members. Share the innumerable small tasks that fill teachers' days. Share your knowledge and ideas with your colleagues; being new means that you will have a fresh approach to old problems.
3. Be open-minded and flexible. Be willing to experiment—it may take a few different approaches to find the right way to accomplish a task. Also, be aware that colleagues may have different goals; if it seems that things are not going as well as you would like, it may be beneficial to stop and clarify everyone's goals. Don't assume that because you are all working on the same project that you have the same goals.

Small differences in perceived goals may result in large differences in strategies and results.
4. Have a sense of humor. Things will go wrong sometimes, and maintaining your perspective is an important part of surviving these times. A new teacher offered the best advice I have heard on this: "Laugh about the day with your team members at the end of every day."

Do note, however, that support and advice from colleagues should never be a substitute for becoming familiar with state, local, district, and school requirements and guidelines. Being aware of what the law requires of you regarding professional practice will allow you to recognize pitfalls and questionable practice.

Unfortunately, one challenge sometimes encountered by new teachers is dealing with ethical and legal issues in the context of working relationships. If colleagues are engaging in practices that you believe to be wrong, it is your responsibility to speak up or, at the very least, to remove yourself from the situation. To dissent from activities or actions that trouble you while maintaining relationships requires strength of character, as well as some subtlety in communication; this can be particularly difficult for new teachers, who often lack experience and confidence. There are situations, as discussed in this text, that require direct action on the part of any teacher; there are also situations that can be handled more informally. You might approach the situation by asking, "Why don't we (fill in the blank), instead?" or "I'm not really comfortable with handling (fill in the blank) this way." Sometimes it is effective simply to have an important task that requires your presence elsewhere. Fortunately, these sorts of difficult situations are the exception rather than the rule.

Remember, you are not in this alone. You have colleagues who represent a tremendous source of information and support on which you may draw, and they have all been beginning teachers. You also have a great deal to offer to your colleagues, even in your first few years, so that the relationships will be mutually beneficial.

GUIDELINES FOR SUCCESS—HOW IMPORTANT ARE TEACHER UNIONS?
Lisa Uphoff

In this day and age when only 1 of every 10 people who work in the private sector belongs to a union or professional association, yet more than 90 percent of all teachers nationwide are members of a union, it is vitally important for a beginning teacher to understand the role her union plays within her school and in her school district. A teachers' union or association is, to borrow a popular phrase, "not your father's union."

To begin, it is absolutely imperative that you, as a new teacher, obtain a copy of your collective-bargaining-agreement (contract), read it, and understand it. The contract is the rulebook. You cannot be successful if you do not understand the rules. In addition to reading the contract, a beginning teacher should introduce himself to his building representative or steward or, in a smaller school district, the officers of the local union and obtain a calendar of union events for the school year. Attend all the meetings and events you can. You will be empowered, meet more of your colleagues, and gain the respect of your peers. Don't be afraid to jump right in and be an active member.

All teachers need to know their Weingarten rights. If you are ever called into a meeting with your principal or supervisor and the meeting is disciplinary in nature, or you feel that discipline could result from this meeting, you have the right to have a union representative present. You must ask for your union representative unless the contract shifts the burden of notice to the employer. Do not be afraid to ask for a union representative. In many schools, the employer will have already notified the union that a meeting is taking place. Unfortunately, the building principal is not always your pal. Protect your rights, and ask for union representation.

Another essential piece of information for every new teacher to acquire is a clear understanding of the district's evaluation plan. Your union can explain your rights under the law and your contract, as well as the evaluation procedure. Are you formally evaluated three times a year? Are you evaluated twice a month? What does the evaluation form look like? Where are completed forms kept, and what other notes or papers are kept on file?

Certification laws and rules vary from state to state. Make sure that the school district has copies of all of your credentials, certificates, teaching endorsements, and so on. Your union may still operate a local professional development committee (LPDC). If so, the LPDC should be given copies of your credentials, and it will assist you with all of your certification questions.

Remember, teaching is a profession, not a temporary stop on the path to another career or a "real job." A successful teacher must be proficient in his subject matter. That is not enough, however. Effective teachers need a repertoire of instructional and classroom management strategies, which can be developed only by on-the-job training. While student teaching is valuable, very often it is not enough. There is no "how-to" manual for teachers. Many fail. Nearly half of new teachers quit within the first five years, and half of those hired in large urban districts leave within three years. Many who quit teaching report being overwhelmed by the task of maintaining discipline and trying to teach at the same time. The union provides professional development designed to improve instructional and classroom management skills. Local unions can offer classes on managing a classroom, teaching reading skills, and many other subjects. Improved skills lead to better teaching. Better teaching leads to greater student achievement.

Many unions provide induction-mentoring programs for their new teachers. Some unions run the entire program, while others work in conjunction with the school district administration. These programs provide support for teachers, increase the teacher's ability to instruct students, improve classroom management skills, help create a collaborative school culture, increase the teacher retention rate, and improve student achievement. In lieu of a formal program, some unions provide avenues for professional partnering.

If your school district or local does not have an induction-mentoring program, it may offer a peer review or peer evaluation program. In 1981, the Toledo Federation of Teachers began offering a peer evaluation program. Every new teacher is evaluated by a team of experienced, respected teachers. The new teachers are observed, advised, and supported by teachers in their areas of expertise. Teachers are professionals who have a vested interest in improving their schools. Well-skilled teachers foster better student performance.

Know your contract. Throughout the 1970s and 1980s, teachers fought and won collective-bargaining rights. Don't take these rights and contractual protections for granted. It's very popular for politicians to lay the blame for all of our social ills at the schoolhouse door. More often than not, the politicians go one step further and lash out at the teachers' unions. Teachers created their unions. It's impossible to separate teachers from their unions. The union is the collective voice of its teachers. Teachers won higher wages, health insurance, a guaranteed pension, and other such benefits because the industrialized workforce had already sought and won these protections. The local members of boards of education believed that teachers deserved these same benefits. One needs only to open the daily newspaper to discover that millions of workers are losing their pension benefits and paying increased health insurance costs throughout the country. If this trend continues, teachers will lose, as well.

Teachers cannot expect to have benefits that the people in their community lack.

It's now more important than ever for teachers to be active, involved, and outspoken. Join your union or professional association. Teachers in a strong union who are protected from arbitrary action by administrators feel more secure and are willing to take chances and make changes that teachers without union protection often resist. Teachers who work in an environment where the union works constructively with the administration as equals and in mutual respect feel more positive about their teaching and their school. Be an active, involved educator. Students will benefit.

CHAPTER 5

Drawing the Line with the Community

Key Concepts

Teacher misconduct
Slander
Defamation
Public forum
Protected speech
Hatch Act
Nonpartisan
Nepotism
Collective bargaining
Good faith
Work stoppage

This chapter will:

1. Describe " whistleblower" protections.
2. Define teacher misconduct.
3. Describe limits on teachers' political speech as imposed by the courts.
4. Define the impact of the Hatch Act on public school educators.
5. Describe the effects of a teacher work stoppage on the community.

HOW CAN TEACHERS GUARD THEIR PERSONAL HONOR?

Teachers are expected by the courts to display personal excellence as well as professional competence, inside and outside the classroom. Teachers, like ministers, are considered role models for the community, modeling a heightened sense of responsibility toward their jobs. Teachers assume a duty or obligation that goes beyond that of other professions, with the exception of the religious ministry. Doctors or lawyers have a professional obligation to improve the welfare of their patients but are not held to account for failing to improve the moral values and/or conduct of those they serve, as teachers and schools are or have been so often been.[1] Teachers must be a fusion of Socrates, Freud, and Einstein, all while displaying the patience and morality of a saint. The task is not impossible; millions of teachers complete their professional responsibilities every day with wit and wisdom.

New teachers often describe the "teachable" moment as the primary reason they came into teaching. That moment when the "light goes off" in the head of the student is often perceived as the most exciting in the teacher-student relationship. No doubt, that one-to-one learning relationship is the elixir that keeps teachers showing up for work. On the other hand, the entire community is very much a part of any learning event. The school is a small part of the greater school district. The district is an integral part of the business, industry, real estate, governmental, and religious organizations that surround the classroom. In truth, the teacher-student relationship is governed by the elected school board and the citizens they represent. The school always completes its mission in a greater context—one that includes thousands of people. The teacher is also a part of the greater community. It is in this community context that the teacher plays an important role.

Teachers are expected to guard their personal honor if they are to remain effective educators in the classroom. If new teachers could be stamped with the word "example" on their foreheads, they might better understand that who they are outside the classroom is critical to their competence inside the classroom. Teachers are held by the courts to a higher standard, because they enjoy the privilege of teaching the nation's youth. Teachers carry both legal and moral authority as they *model* moral behavior and act in such a way that leads youth in a positive and beneficial direction. Many education ethics codes describe teachers as holding a "public trust and responsibility that requires the highest ideals of professional service." Many states include in the phrase "to be found of high moral character" in the teacher licensure certificate. American civil and criminal courts have consistently held teachers to a "higher standard" than other professions because they have the high privilege of working with the nation's youth.[2] No excuses can be given for those who transgress societal mandates or violate accepted professional standards of practice.

Who teachers are *in their personal lives* outside class matters a great deal to the greater community. In fact, many teachers have been released from their employment due after the community has lost confidence in their teaching. A teacher may be fired or nonrenewed for "diminished effectiveness" as a teacher or for exhibiting a "disturbing influence on students" as a result of rumors in the greater community. Nonrenewal of teaching contacts may be upheld by courts depending on the wording of the school district's policy, whether it has complied with due process requirements, and after a substantive review of the evidence. A district must have clearly determined criteria for not renewing a teacher's contact.[3] Negative community reaction to a teacher infraction is considered an indicator of "diminished effectiveness" in the classroom. Teachers must be aware that their actions resound loudly in their community—for good or for ill.

WHAT IS TEACHER MISCONDUCT?

Teacher misconduct is tightly defined by state statutes, state criminal codes, and state department of education ethics codes for professional educators and school administrators. Teachers who are involved in any misconduct may face certification suspension, criminal investigation, and loss of employment. Teacher misconduct may involve any criminal action, such as theft, sexual misconduct, child abuse, abuse of substances, embezzlement of funds, or assault and battery, or a noncriminal action such as criticizing the school administration in public, abusing district sick and personal leave, or failing to censor student materials. The range for doing the wrong thing is quite broad. The community will always have a strong reaction to teachers who violate the professional persona.

Community standards vary, depending on the community. The same behavior that might get a teacher released from his employment in rural Iowa might not even be noticed in Chicago. Certainly the most glaring example of differing community standards relates to teacher morality. A pregnant, unwed teacher may not be censured in a large urban district. On the other hand, small communities may have very vocal citizens who take great notice of such a situation. Teachers who engage in adultery may also have their "fitness to teach" questioned by boards of education.[4] Finally, teachers who have had offenses expunged from their criminal record may be fired because the expungement did "not erase the fact that they had committed the act, nor did it erase the moral turpitude of the teacher's conduct."[5] Community reactions to any spot on the reputation of those it entrusts to care for young children are often vehement and rarely informed. On the other hand, a surefire way for a teacher to be shown the door is to become involved with a student in a romantic relationship.

All teachers should be aware that teacher sexual misconduct is an immediate career killer—expect no second chances. The idea a teacher would sexually abuse a child is an anathema in all schools and communities in the United States. It goes without saying such misconduct is utterly without legal defense and is also a felony crime. All teachers would be well advised to know how to be proactive in their interactions with potentially problematic students and to avoid any situations that could lead to accusations of impropriety.

Wrongful allegations of teacher sexual misconduct are made every day. The teachers involved rarely get an opportunity to prove the student wrong, as the rush to judgment in the community is too strong to be resisted. The teacher usually leaves the district as quickly as possible, even if completely innocent.

Remember, even if the allegation of misconduct is proven wrong, the district may still end the teacher's employment due to a perceived "diminished effectiveness" or for exhibiting a "disturbing influence on students." Teachers serve as role models for pupils, and school boards expect them to display high moral standards to maintain that important status.[6]

Case in Point

In re Heather B., Md. No. 90, Sept. Term 2001, June 7, 2002

A volleyball coach, a 30-year veteran of the classroom, was alleged to have "leered" into a girl's locker room and watched seven members of the team as they dressed. The coach retired quickly, weeks before the girls recanted their accusation. The blame for the concocted charges came to rest on a single student irked at a practice reprimand from the coach. School and police officials charged her with falsely reporting a crime. The juvenile court judge imposed a small fine and community service time for the girl. Her attorney argued that the punishment should be retracted, because the girl did not file the false report; the school district did. No punishment was ever given to the student. The coach sold his home and left the community under intense pressure.

Kimble v. Worth County R-III Board of Education, 669 S.W.2d 949 (Mo. Ct. App. 1984)

A teacher with a continuing contract was terminated because of three instances of petty theft of school property—$20 in cash, a teapot, and a set of schoolbooks. The court refused to reinstate her, accepting that she faced a "reduced efficiency to teach."

Sullivan v. Meade County Independent School Dist., 530 F2d 799, S.Dak. (1976)

A single teacher from New York City accepted a teaching position in a small rural town in South Dakota. When she allowed her boyfriend to move into her mobile home, the school district dismissed her on the ground that her personal conduct was detrimental to the students in her care. More than 140 residents signed a community petition demanding that she be removed from the school. She responded with a lawsuit alleging that her constitutional rights had been violated. The courts disagreed with the teacher, declaring "that the state is entitled to require teachers to maintain a properly moral environment in the interest of the well-being of youth."

Talk It Over

An elementary school teacher is accused of shoplifting a small item at the local grocery store. The teacher is arrested and released. The following day, the school district places the teacher on unpaid administrative leave. Within days, the teacher resigns her faculty position. The police drop the theft charge because the item taken was a small pack of chewing gum.

Best-Practice Overview

Always do the right thing. Mom's best advice still proves valuable for teachers. In education, the perception is the reality. The community expects teachers to be above reproach in their private lives, as well as in the school setting.

When teachers suspected of misconduct are released from a school district (especially teachers who have an unblemished reputation in the community), often an emotional tug-of-war begins in the media. Students and parents come to the teacher's aid to protest her treatment by the school administration. Headlines abound. Unfortunately, this adds fuel to the fire in the local boardroom. The school administration cannot share its information or factual evidence with the media or community members because of the possibility that the teacher will accuse it of slander or defamation. The only recourse the administration has is to give no comment to the media. This practice, of course, inflames the community members, who may be determined to regain the faculty member's position or exoneration. It is a no-win situation for school administration, with the teacher caught in the middle.

A school board will always err on the side of safety; that is, the faculty member will be placed on administrative leave (paid or unpaid) and barred from entering to the campus or contact with faculty or students until the investigation is completed. Accused teachers simply disappear from the school. School districts are under no state mandate to finish their investigations. In some cases, the school district may reopen the investigation years later, when new information becomes available. The faculty member who is reinstated may have to teach under a sword of Damocles from year to year. The best advice is not to get into such a situation. Teach wisely and live wisely. Remember, community standards are the legal standards for teachers' lifestyle.

ARE THERE LIMITATIONS ON TEACHERS' POLITICAL OPINIONS OR THEIR RIGHT TO HOLD PUBLIC OFFICE?

The following four statements are true:

Teachers are often at odds with administrative decisions made by school district officials. Teachers are often at odds with decisions made by local and federal governmental bodies. Teachers are often at odds with decisions made by community members.

Teachers can be very vocal in their disagreement!

How free are teachers to criticize local or school district officials? First Amendment freedoms guarantee all citizens the right to freely speak about their political opinions, unrestricted by employment or party affiliation.[7] When teachers have taken freedom-of-speech issues to court, judges have been very careful in their decisions because a teacher is a public employee. Much depends on the forum and the issues.

The Supreme Court in the precedent-setting *Pickering v. Board of Education* case established a three-part test for determining whether public speech by government employees is protected. Open-forum comments must:

1. Relate to matters of public concern.
2. Involve issues that outweigh the government's interest in efficient public service.
3. Include comments expressed primarily in the employee's role as a citizen, not the speaker's position as an employee.[8]

A teacher may speak in a public forum, such as an open call-in radio show, through a written letter to a newspaper, or at a public meeting (e.g., "open comments" time at a school board meeting). Again, the court has qualified its protection of teachers' comments made in an open forum. Teacher speech is protected if the teacher's comments are factual and are not made with reckless disregard of the truth. Courts have been clear to support teachers' political activities and expression of political opinions when those activities have stayed clearly within the scope of good citizenship.

A teacher may not use the classroom to criticize the school administration. Courts have ruled that a classroom is not a public forum but an arena in which the teacher serves as a clear representative of the school board that employs him and in which the teacher enjoys undue influence on students and parents.[9] Media interviews granted by teachers also are not considered open forums, as teachers are considered employees of the district.[10] Furthermore, any materials posted on teacher bulletin boards or hallway displays are considered to be under the control of the school and do not represent the equivalent of free speech.[11] The California courts have agreed that teachers may not wear political campaign buttons in the classroom, as this practice would place undue influence on students.[12] Remember, employee insubordination is not protected by the First Amendment guarantee of free speech.[13]

Finally, an important point needs to be made about private speech—it is not protected. What you say in private conversations regarding the school district or administration polices will not be protected in court.[14] Simple complaints about the day-to-day administration of the schools will not qualify as protected speech. School administrators must put the mission of schools and the pubic service they provide to the community first in determining all school policies. That requirement alone may limit teachers' political activities within school hours. As U.S. Supreme Court Justice Holmes stated, in 1892, "The petitioner may have a constitutional right to talk politics, but he has no constitutional right to be a policeman."[15]

Teachers are involved people, in their communities and in their school districts. Could a teacher run for a seat on the school board of the district in which he is employed?

The Hatch Act prohibits public employees from campaigning or running for public office in a partisan election—one in which candidates represent major political parties.[16] School board elections are nonpartisan elections. The courts have imposed three tests to determine whether teachers, as employees of a local governmental entity, may run for public office:

- *An incompatibility-of-office provision.* That test asks whether the teacher can complete the duties assigned by the school district and the demands of the public office at the same time. Teachers may not maintain their employment while holding office. Teachers who run for state legislatures or local city councils may have to take an unpaid leave of absence while they hold office.

- *A conflict-of-interest provision.* A conflict of interest could result for a teacher who sits on a school board in the district in which she is employed. On the other hand, teachers may serve on the board of a school district in which they are not employed.[17]

- *A separation-of-the-branches- of-government provision.* Usually teachers would not be serving as mayor and as judge at the same time.

Finally, state nepotism laws may prohibit teachers from sitting on school boards in districts that employ a near relative of the teacher.

Teachers may campaign for other political candidates if campaigning does not:

- Happen during work hours.
- Take place in the classroom.
- Require the employee to use her position to influence the outcome of the election.
- Interfere with the employee's job performance.

Teachers who take a stand against wasteful, fraudulent, or dangerous actions by the local school board are protected by federal and state law under so-called whistleblower immunity. Whistleblower statutes are on the books in 40 states and are included in much federal legislation, such as Title IX. Whistleblower protection offers an umbrella of immunity (including protection against adverse employment actions such as termination) to teachers or school administrators who, in good faith, report a violation of law, financial waste, or a specific danger to the public health and safety that is being committed by their school board.[18]

Case in Point

Los Angeles Teacher Union v. Los Angeles City Board of Education, 455 P.2d 827 (Calif. 1969)

A school board attempted to restrict teachers from circulating a petition against the state legislature's plans to cut back funding for education. The court found that the petitions did not constitute a substantial disruption of or material interference with school activities. Furthermore, the courts declared that "teachers like, others, have the right to speak freely and effectively on public questions as well as the inseparable and cognate right to petition the government for a redress of grievances. They do not shed these rights at the schoolhouse gate."

*Childers v. Independent School District No. 1, 676 F2d 1338
(10th Cir. 1982)*

Teachers who actively supported a candidate (who lost) for the school board found themselves out of summer employment. The teachers were supported by the courts, which admonished the board against dismissing or reprimanding teachers for engaging in political activities within the scope of their citizenship.

Talk It Over

A high school social studies class begins a project to educate the local community about the school board members and their occupations. The students find out that one member owns, but does not run, a local liquor store. The teacher knows that this conservative community is not aware of the connection between the school board member and "Swinger's Drinks." What should the teacher do with the information found by the students?

Best-Practice Overview

Teaching is not the occupation to select if you want to show blatant disregard for social norms, community standards, or employer policies. All professional teachers are highly educated people. Along with that education may come an elevated sense of importance. Many teachers become adversarial in their employment with their school district. Teachers who find themselves in combat with school administrators are on very tenuous grounds in terms of their employment. When teachers move from personal opinion to personal vendetta, trouble begins in the school.

The First Amendment protects teachers' comments made in an open forum, not those uttered in a faculty lounge. Remember, teachers may speak about anything outside of school—so take any conflicts through proper channels or take the issue outside the school campus. Teacher speech centered on issues that affect the school mission or the greater community is appropriate, if expressed within the teacher's role as a citizen. Finally, be involved in local politics. Set an example of active citizenship for students to emulate. Teachers make thoughtful and effective members of local offices and consider the welfare of young people in all decisions. The public arena needs ethical and educated people to serve as leaders.

WHAT IS A TEACHER WORK STOPPAGE?

A wide range of practices exists among the 50 states regarding school employment practices. According to the National Education Association, approximately 70 percent of the states have statutes that provide for good-faith bargaining between local school boards and bargaining groups. Some states leave negotiations with teachers or their bargaining representatives to the discretion of local boards, while others provide for bargaining rights that compare to those in the private sector (for example, the practice of imposing "fair share" dues for nonmembers of local associations). In other states (e.g., Texas, Georgia, Virginia, and North Carolina), court orders or state statutes prohibit any collective bargaining. These states encourage a "meet and confer" practice between members of local school boards and members of professional associations.[19] The local school board is an arm of state government and must represent the people in all decisions. Ultimately, no agent can decide for the board what a negotiation settlement will be; only the board has full lawful authority to accept or reject any contract agreement made by a negotiation team or superintendent.

Teacher work stoppages cause many problems. One thing that can strike fear in the heart of student teachers is the chance that their capstone experience may be interrupted by a teacher work stoppage and that they may be caught in the middle of it. Fear of pressures by the administration to continue to teach, fear of pressures from cooperating teachers to participate in the stoppage, fear that their college will make them cross a union line—all these can overwhelm student teachers.

No less real is the concern felt by other members of the community. Parents seem powerless to bring the school administrators and teachers together. Working parents scramble for safe childcare to take the place of school supervision. Parents may also be concerned about graduation requirements and missed athletic contests. They fear any interruption in the school calendar that will affect their children adversely. Feeling a common bond with their child's teachers, parents seldom side with the school board.

School administrators have great problems holding a faculty together before a stoppage and an impossible task after a stoppage. The safety of the school pupils left with ill-prepared substitute teachers causes liability concerns. Dealing with vendors who may support the union line and not deliver bread and milk to the school kitchen may be difficult at best. Teachers lose valuable instructional time, miss the salary deducted from their paychecks for days not worked, and may have to face adamant parents on the union line. And always, the potential for violence is present.

Teacher work stoppages are extremely serious and are seen as such by the nation's courts system.

School boards are required by state law to bargain in "good faith"—that means with no malice and with all intent to come to an agreement. Teacher unions are also required by state law to bargain in good faith. When negotiations break down, the courts must decide what to do. Many cases have dealt with violations of state law that define the rights and duties of those engaged in collective bargaining. Violations on either side may include these:

- Denial by the employer of the use of facilities (e.g., teacher lockouts).
- Denial of school resources for union activity (e.g., refusal to allow unions to post information or use district mail).
- Attempts to coerce employees to vote a certain way in an election (e.g., by promising a change in school teaching loads).
- Use of intimidation and harassment (e.g., nonrenewal of union building representatives).
- Use of lapses in medical or life insurance coverage by the employer to force teachers into an agreement.
- Refusal to bargain (e.g., by not attending scheduled negotiations attempts).
- Refusal to implement a negotiated agreement (e.g., by not implementing school calendar holidays voted by the teachers).
- Refusal to enter into a mediation/resolution agreement (e.g., by opposing intervention by state agencies such as the public employment relations boards or the fair practices board).
- Engaging in an unlawful strike, such as a sickout.
- Termination of employment (e.g., nonrenewal for teachers who participated in the work stoppage).[20]

Clearly, the opportunity exists for both sides to violate the boundary of reason and prudent action. In fact, the scars left by a teacher work stoppage may last for years and set an adversarial tone between school administration and teachers that remains evident for decades.

Many states have laws against teacher strikes on the ground that public employees cannot stop providing essential public services. In *Wheeler v. Natalie*, the court declared the premise behind the decision to bar teachers from striking:

The state has a compelling interest that one of its most precious assets—its youth- have the opportunity to drink at the font of knowledge so they may be nurtured and develop into the responsible citizens of tomorrow, No one has the right to turn off the fountain spigot and keep it in a closed position. Likewise the equal protection afforded by the fourteenth amendment does not guarantee perfect equality. There is a difference between a private employee and a public employee, such as a teacher who plays such an important part in enabling the state to discharge its constitutional responsibility. The need of preventing governmental paralysis justifies the "no strike" distinction for the private sector with our labor force.[21]

Even in states that allow teachers to strike, the courts may still issue an injunction ordering the teachers back to work if the strike presents a significant threat to public safety or is otherwise seriously detrimental to the public welfare. As a result, if teacher strikes are called, most occur at the start of the school year or at the very end to minimize disruption to the academic year.

Case in Point

Hortonville Joint School District No. 1 v. Hortonville Education Association, 426 U.S. 482 (1976)

A Wisconsin state statue prohibited teachers from striking. This school district was embroiled in a prolonged work stoppage, and the school board held a hearing for the striking teachers and voted to terminate their employment because they had violated their individual employment contracts. The court held that a local school board can conduct a hearing to terminate teachers who are striking illegally—even though it was negotiating labor questions at the same time.

Talk It Over

A principal calls all first-year teachers into his office to inform them that the teacher union may be on the verge of a work stoppage. He reminds them that they are on provisional contracts and therefore may not be returning to the school district the following year. He wants to know which of the first-year teachers are members of the teacher association currently involved in collective negotiations. What message does this action send to the teachers?

Best-Practice Overview

Voting for a work stoppage is a personal decision. No one comes into the profession for the tremendous remuneration. The fact remains that teachers should have some measure of self-determination as professionals. That expectation alone may indeed encourage teachers to participate in a work stoppage. On the other hand, school board politics can become very divisive and destructive to a district faculty. One or two board members (who may be gone from the board in a few years) can effectively hold up good-faith negotiations with the entire teacher workforce. Some districts, strapped for state funds, have locked teachers out of their classrooms until they accept a lower salary structure. There are no easy answers to the question of whether teacher work stoppages are acceptable. Readers are encouraged to become very involved in their home school district and to raise their voices on the side of fairness and moderation. Teaching is an honorable profession, and the fact that many of America's teachers can qualify for state food stamps is a national disgrace. Three great practices for new and veteran teachers alike: be informed, listen to all sides, and vote your conscience.

HOW MAY TEACHERS USE THE MEDIA?

The TV news reporter approached first-year teachers as they exited an orientation session days before the start of school. "Well, how was your first day as a teacher in the district? Do you feel prepared?" the reporter asked. One young teacher replied, "This was a total waste of my time. I could have been working in my classroom to get ready."

Certainly, this reply was not a very good way to make a great first impression on school board members, school administrators, and fellow faculty members. To borrow from law enforcement, "What you say to the media will be held against you."

Education news stories often take a back seat to all other news. In fact, it requires a very slow news day for any coverage of schools to be considered of any importance, even at the level of "human interest." The few exceptions to this rule include any stories that hint at teacher sexual misconduct; a funding scandal, low standardized test scores; or infighting within school boards. A threatened teacher strike may not appear on the front page until the event actually happens. Unfortunately, the topic of "schools" is not headline news—when things are going well.

School districts often hire public relations or communications people to handle all in-house communications (i.e., newsletters), as well as to respond to any inquiries by the media.

School districts have specific polices for the accurate distribution of news connected to school district activities, including athletics. In many cases, teachers are unaware of those policies and attempt to use the media to focus attention on their pet peeves. When teachers provide information that reflects negatively on the school district, they are in violation of school district policy—the same policy they have been hired to represent.

School administrators serve as the sole media contact when teachers want news coverage for classroom projects, fundraising, or community projects. The superintendent's office will provide media "talking points" to the school administrator closest to the event. Then the administrator will be required to stay close to the approved information. Federal law prohibits media from talking or taking pictures of minor children without parental permission, so the administrator—not the teacher—must contact the parents of students selected to appear with media representatives. Since the attack at Columbine High School, all districts have emergency plans that include information and calling plans to inform faculty of school emergencies. Every effective emergency plan has an administrative directive that gives specific persons permission to speak with the media. Anyone else is strictly prohibited from providing public comment. The only exception is for coaches, who may need to contact news media to report game scores and outstanding players for local news coverage. Simply said, teachers may not speak with the media without prior approval from school district administration.

Case in Point

Wheeler v. Natalie, 178 F.Supp.2d 407 (S.D.N.Y. 2001)

A clerical employee of a school district who often spoke about school issues on a local radio show was not hired for a new position in the school district.

She claimed that the comments she had made as a show participant had angered the school district superintendent, who then instructed his other employees to monitor the show. When the district hired another employee for the position, the clerk filed suit. The board prevailed in the suit because no direct connection could be made between the clerk's comments and the superintendent's choice to hire another person.

Talk It Over

A band director, angry about a halftime dispute with the football coach, calls a local radio show to report the free landscaping provided to the coach by school horticultural classes. Newspaper reporters overhear the broadcast accusation and speed to the coach's front lawn to take pictures of the shrubbery provided at taxpayers' expense. How would this situation impact the community confidence level regarding the schools?

Best-Practice Overview

- Imagine a school district in which any school employee is free to call media personnel and air any small grievance, truthful or not.
- Imagine elementary-level students who have their pictures in local newspapers. Perhaps those students were placed in foster homes for protection from abusive parents and are now being paraded before all eyes.
- Imagine faculty rivalries and disputes used as fodder for newspaper coverage.

The danger and chaos resulting from these events would be overwhelming. Teachers must not take media "photo opportunities" into their own hands. They must be guided by school administrators, who have a greater awareness of the law and of privacy requirements. School districts have policies that govern media releases. Be sure to remember that teachers have a contractual obligation to follow school district policy when dealing with media personnel. In sum, all interactions with the local media must be cleared with the building principal well before the teacher invites the media into the classroom to cover student projects and activities. Parents must be given clear warning of such visits and must be allowed to opt their child out of any photographs. Not every one is happy to have her child's picture featured in the local news. If the media have cleared all interviews with the school administration and one teacher is encouraged to grant an interview, that teacher must be sure to weigh her words very clearly and not to express negative thoughts about her employer.

Appendix: Ethic Codes of Educators

NATIONAL EDUCATION ASSOCIATION

Code of Ethics of the Education Profession

Principle I

Commitment to the Student. The educator strives to help each student realize his or her potential as a worthy and effective member of society. The educator therefore works to stimulate the spirit of inquiry, the acquisition of knowledge and understanding, and the thoughtful formulation of worthy goals.

In fulfillment of the obligation to the student, the educator—

1. Shall not unreasonably restrain the student from independent action in the pursuit of learning.
2. Shall not unreasonably deny the student's access to varying points of view.
3. Shall not deliberately suppress or distort subject matter relevant to the student's progress.
4. Shall make reasonable effort to protect the student from conditions harmful to learning or to health and safety.
5. Shall not intentionally expose the student to embarrassment or disparagement.
6. Shall not on the basis of race, color, creed, sex, national origin, marital status, political or religious beliefs, family, social or cultural background, or sexual orientation, unfairly—

   a. Exclude any student from participation in any program
   b. Deny benefits to any student
   c. Grant any advantage to any student

7. Shall not use professional relationships with students for private advantage.

8. Shall not disclose information about students obtained in the course of professional service unless disclosure serves a compelling professional purpose or is required by law.

Principle II

Commitment to the Profession. The education profession is vested by the public with a trust and responsibility requiring the highest ideals of professional service.

In the belief that the quality of the services of the education profession directly influences the nation and its citizens, the educator shall exert every effort to raise professional standards, to promote a climate that encourages the exercise of professional judgment, to achieve conditions that attract persons worthy of the trust to careers in education, and to assist in preventing the practice of the profession by unqualified persons.

In fulfillment of the obligation to the profession, the educator—

1. Shall not in an application for a professional position deliberately make a false statement or fail to disclose a material fact related to competency and qualifications.
2. Shall not misrepresent his/her professional qualifications.
3. Shall not assist any entry into the profession of a person known to be unqualified in respect to character, education, or other relevant attribute.
4. Shall not knowingly make a false statement concerning the qualifications of a candidate for a professional position.
5. Shall not assist a noneducator in the unauthorized practice of teaching.
6. Shall not disclose information about colleagues obtained in the course of professional service unless disclosure serves a compelling professional purpose or is required by law.
7. Shall not knowingly make false or malicious statements about a colleague.
8. Shall not accept any gratuity, gift, or favor that might impair or appear to influence professional decisions or action.

AMERICAN ASSOCIATION OF SCHOOL ADMINISTRATORS

Code of Ethics for School Administrators

An educational administrator's professional behavior must conform to an ethical code. The code must be idealistic and at the same time practical, so that it can apply reasonably to all educational administrators. To these ends, the administrator subscribes to the following statements of standards.

The educational administrator:

1. Makes the wellbeing of students the fundamental value of all decision making and actions.
2. Fulfills professional responsibilities with honesty and integrity.
3. Supports the principle of due process and protects the civil and human rights of all individuals.
4. Obeys local, state, and national laws and does not knowingly join or support organization that advocate, directly or indirectly, the overthrow of the government.

5. Implements the governing board of education's policies and administrative rules and regulations.
6. Pursues appropriate measures to correct those laws, policies, and regulations that are not consistent with sound educational goals.
7. Avoids using positions for personal gain through political, social, religious, economic, or other influence.
8. Accepts academic degrees or professional certification only from duly accredited institutions.
9. Maintains the standards and seeks to improve the effectiveness of the profession through research and continuing professional development.
10. Honors all contracts until fulfillment or release.

INTERNATIONAL READING ASSOCIATION

Code of Ethics

The members of the International Reading Association form a group of professional persons committed to the development of society through teaching, professional services, research, and publication. The members of this group are committed to values that are the foundation of a democratic society—freedom to teach, write, and study in an atmosphere conducive to the best interests of the profession. The best interests of the public, the profession, and the individuals concerned should be of primary consideration in recommending candidates for degrees, positions, advancements, the recognition of professional activity, and for certification in those areas where certification exists.

Ethical Standards in Professional Relationships

• It is the obligation of all members of the International Reading Association to observe the Code of Ethics of the organization and to act accordingly so as to advance the status and prestige of the Association and of the profession as a whole. Members should assist in establishing the highest professional standards for reading programs and services, and should enlist support for these through dissemination of pertinent information to the public.

• It is the obligation of all members to maintain relationships with other professional persons, striving for harmony, avoiding personal controversy, encouraging cooperative effort, and making known the obligations and services rendered by professionals in reading.

Ethical Standards for Reading Professionals

• Professionals in reading must possess suitable qualifications for engaging in consulting, diagnostic, or remedial work. Unqualified persons should not engage in such activities except under the direct supervision of one who is properly qualified. Professional intent and the welfare of the person seeking services should govern all consulting or clinical activities such as counseling, administering diagnostic tests, or providing remediation. It is the duty of the professional in reading to keep relationships with clients and interested persons on a professional level.

- Information derived from consulting and/or professional services should be regarded as confidential. Expressed consent of persons involved should be secured before releasing information to outside agencies.
- Professionals in reading should recognize the boundaries of their competence and should not offer services that fail to meet professional standards established by other disciplines. They should be free, however, to give assistance in other areas in which they are qualified.
- Reading clinics and/or reading professionals offering services should refrain from guaranteeing easy solutions or favorable outcomes as a result of their work, and their advertising should be consistent with that of allied professions. They should not accept for remediation any persons who are unlikely to benefit from their instruction, and they should work to accomplish the greatest possible improvement in the shortest time. Fees, if charged, should be agreed on in advance and should be charged in accordance with an established set of rates commensurate with that of other professions.

NATIONAL CATHOLIC EDUCATIONAL ASSOCIATION

Code of Ethics for the Catholic School Teacher

Principle I

Commitment to the Student. In fulfilling our obligation to the student, we are called to:

1. Help students see the relevance of a Christian value system in their daily lives.
2. Help students learn to relate human culture and knowledge to the news of salvation.
3. Show Christian concern about the joys and problems of each student.
4. Speak with charity and justice about students even when called upon to discuss sensitive matters.
5. Work with students in preparing liturgies, paraliturgies, and other religious programs.
6. Respect confidential information concerning students and their homes.
7. Plan appropriate service projects for students that will develop their sense of responsibility to the community.
8. Enable students to grow in a sense of self-worth and accountability by selecting activities which promote the positive self-concept as becomes a maturing Christian.
9. Develop the students' knowledge and understanding of the subject(s) for which we are responsible without suppression or distortion.
10. Refuse remuneration for tutoring students assigned to our classes and reject any other use of our students for personal financial gain.

Principle II

Commitment to Parents. We are called to assist these parents in fulfilling their obligation for the Christian formation and education of their child; therefore, we will:

1. Respect parents' fundamental human right to know, to understand, and to share in decisions that affect the education of their child by

a. assuring parents of a commitment to ongoing education as a professional educator and informing them, upon request, of educational qualifications.

b. keeping parents apprised of the curriculum and method of instruction.

c. providing opportunities for parents to help shape classroom and school policies and keeping them well informed regarding all current policies.

2. Develop educational programs and activities to enhance family life as well as the home–school relationship.

3. Respect any confidential information which parents share.

4. Report to parents their child's progress regularly and as needed, in a spirit of charity, with professional accuracy and honesty.

Principle III

In fulfilling our obligation to our apostolic profession, we are called to:

1. Promote the peace of Christ in the world by:

a. modeling peaceful solutions to community conflicts.

b. encouraging a spirit of cooperation and avoiding the extremes in competition.

c. developing skills which will enable students to interact with society for a better world.

2. Cooperate wholeheartedly in the continued building of parish life and spirit by:

a. emphasizing the integral nature of the Catholic school within the parish and community.

b. assisting communication concerning parish resources, needs, and events.

c. modeling active participation in one's own parish.

3. Develop student potential for constructive Christian leadership within the American democracy by:

a. ensuring an adequate understanding of history and its lessons.

b. providing opportunities for taking responsible moral positions on current issues.

c. offering instruction and practice in leadership skills.

4. Contribute to the well-being of the area in which the school is located by:

a. reflecting the philosophy of the school in one's attitudes and actions.

b. manifesting respect and appreciation for the work of educators in other schools and systems.

c. encouraging in students a respect for the person and property of their neighbors.

d. avoiding inappropriate school activities that disturb the peace and order of the community.

Principle IV

Commitment to the Profession. In fulfilling our responsibilities as professional educators we are called to:

1. Maintain professional standards by:

   a. preserving the reputations of colleagues, administrators, and students.
   b. safeguarding the exchange of confidential information.
   c. refusing to use the classroom to further personal ends through the sale of any goods, products, or publications.
   d. refraining from using the school as a platform for one's own beliefs which are not in accord with the school philosophy or Church teaching.
   e. overseeing the duties of nonprofessionals, making sure they assume only those responsibilities appropriate to their role.
   f. assisting in the orientation of educators new to a position and/or school.
   g. considering the obligations of the teaching contract as binding in a most serious manner, conscientiously fulfilling the contract.
   h. terminating unexpired contracts only because of serious reasons, with the consent of both parties, and after sufficient notice.
   i. upholding the authority of the school when communicating with parents, students, and civic community.
   j. presenting honest, accurate professional qualifications of self and colleagues when required for professional reasons.

2. Seek and encourage persons who live a life consonant with Gospel values and Catholic Church teachings to pursue the apostolate of teaching by:

   a. modeling the faith life and witnessing to the Faith Community on the parish, diocesan, national, and world levels.
   b. exemplifying the teachings of Jesus Christ by dealing with children and adults in true love and justice.
   c. exhibiting knowledge of the Church documents, especially "To Teach as Jesus Did," "Sharing the Light of Faith," and "The Catholic School."

AMERICAN LIBRARY ASSOCIATION

Statement on Professional Ethics, 1981

Code of Ethics

I. Librarians must provide the highest level of service through appropriate and usefully organized collections, fair and equitable circulation and service policies, and skillful, accurate, unbiased, and courteous responses to all requests for assistance.

II. Librarians must resist all efforts by groups or individuals to censor library materials.

III. Librarians must protect each user's right to privacy with respect to information sought or received, and materials consulted, borrowed, or acquired.

IV. Librarians must adhere to the principles of due process and equality of opportunity in peer relationships and personnel actions.

V. Librarians must distinguish clearly in their actions and statements between their personal philosophies and attitudes and those of an institution or professional body.

VI. Librarians must avoid situations in which personal interests might be served or financial benefits gained at the expense of library users, colleagues, or the employing institution.

DIVISION FOR EARLY CHILDHOOD (DEC) OF THE COUNCIL FOR EXCEPTIONAL CHILDREN (CEC)

Code of Ethics

1. Demonstrate the highest standards of personal integrity, truthfulness, and honesty in all our professional activities in order to inspire the confidence and trust of the public and those with whom we work;

2. Demonstrate our respect and concern for children and families, colleagues, and others with whom we work, honoring their beliefs, values, customs, and culture;

3. Demonstrate our respect for families in their task of nurturing their children and support them in achieving the outcomes they desire for themselves and their children;

4. Demonstrate, in our behavior and language, that we respect and appreciate the unique value and human potential of each child;

5. Strive for personal professional excellence, seeking new information, using new information and ideas, and responding openly to the suggestions of others;

6. Encourage the professional development of our colleagues and those seeking to enter fields related to early childhood special education, early intervention, and personnel preparation, offering guidance, assistance, support, and mentorship to others without the burden of professional competition;

7. Ensure that programs and services we provide are based on law as well as a current knowledge of and recommended practice in early childhood special education, early intervention, and personnel preparation;

8. Serve as an advocate for children with special needs and their families and for the professionals who serve them in our communities working with those who make the policy and programmatic decisions that enhance or depreciate the quality of their lives;

9. Oppose any discrimination because of race, color, religion, sex, sexual orientation, national origin, political affiliation, disability, age, or marital status in all aspects of personnel action and service delivery;

10. Protect the privacy and confidentiality of information regarding children and families, colleagues, and students; and

11. Reflect our commitment to the Division for Early Childhood and to its adopted policies and positions.

NATIONAL ASSOCIATION OF SCHOOL PSYCHOLOGISTS

Principles for Professional Ethics

I. Professional Competency

    a. The school psychologist strives to maintain the highest standards of service by an objective collecting of appropriate data and information necessary to effectively work with the student. In conducting a psychological evaluation, due consideration is given to individual integrity and individual differences by the selection and use of appropriate procedures and assessment techniques.

  b. The school psychologist is guided by an awareness of the intimate nature of the process which may entail an examination of the personal aspects of the life of an individual.

  c. The school psychologist is prudently aware of the possible influence personal biases and professional limitations impose on their ability to serve a student, and of the continuing obligation for protecting the privacy and confidence of the student.

II. Professional Responsibility

  a. The school psychologist defines life direction and the nature of personal loyalties, objectives, and competencies, and advises and informs all persons concerned of these commitments. Students are faithfully and objectively represented to teachers, parents, and other professionals, as well as to the student.

  b. The school psychologist insists upon collecting data for an evaluation in a manner that lends itself to maximum verification, includes relevant information, and is based on assessment techniques which are appropriate for the client.

  c. When reporting data which are to be representative of the student, the school psychologist makes certain that life information is in such form and style as to assure that the recipient of the report will be able to give maximum assistance to the client. The emphasis is on the interpretation and organization rather than the simple passing along of test scores and will include a professional appraisal of life degree of reliance which can be placed on the information.

  d. Where a situation occurs in which there are divided or conflicting interests (as parent-school-student), the school psychologist is responsible for working out a pattern of action which assures mutual benefit and protection of rights for all concerned.

III. Professional Relationships with Students

  a. The school psychologist recognizes their obligation to the student and respects the student's right of choice to enter or to participate in services voluntarily.

  b. The school psychologist explains to the student who the psychologist is, what the psychologist does, and why the student is being seen.

  c. The school psychologist informs the student of their rationale of sharing information. The course of action proposed takes into account the rights of the student, the rights or the parent, the responsibilities of the school personnel, and the expanding self-independence and mature status of the student.

  d. The school psychologist discusses with the student all contemplated changes in status and plans which are suggested as a result of psychological study.

  e. The student is referred when a condition is identified which is outside the treatment competencies or scope of the school psychologist.

IV. Professional Relationships with the School

  a. The school psychologist interprets professional services provided in order to ensure a realistic picture of what psychological services entail.

b. The school psychologist's concern for protecting the interests and rights of students is communicated to the school administration and staff.

c. The school psychologist communicates findings and recommendations in language readily understood by the school staff.

d. The school psychologist is obligated to ascertain that psychoeducational information reaches responsible and authorized persons and is adequately interpreted for their use in helping the pupil.

V. Professional Relationships with Parents

a. The school psychologist recognizes the importance of parental support and seeks to obtain this by assuring that there is parent contact prior to seeing the student.

b. The school psychologist insures that recommendations and plans for assisting the child are discussed with the parent.

c. The school psychologist informs the parent of the nature of records made of parent conferences and evaluations of the child.

VI. Principles Governing Relationships with Other Professions

a. The school psychologist explains and interprets professional competencies of the school psychologist to other professionals so that assignment of services can be made clearly and unambiguously.

b. The school psychologist maintains the skills and ethics of the profession when cooperating with other professionals.

c. The school psychologist is obligated to have prior knowledge of the competency and qualifications of the referral resource.

d. The school psychologist recognizes that various techniques and methods are shared with other professional groups.

VII. Principles Pertaining to Relationships with the Community

a. The school psychologist acts as a resource person to establish and maintain the availability of adequate psychological services and also recognizes the right of individuals to avail themselves of such services at their own discretion and free of coercion.

NATIONAL COUNCIL OF TEACHERS OF MATHEMATICS

A Professional Oath for Mathematics Teachers

I recognize that teaching mathematics is a privilege that comes with responsibilities. I know that I, like all mathematics teachers, must observe the core values of the profession. These values center on the duty to educate people and eliminate ignorance. Students are my first concern. I promise that I will use my knowledge to benefit students. I will listen to them, work with them, and provide them with the best education that I can. I will be honest, respectful, and compassionate toward them and will do my best to educate them all.

I will make every effort to ensure that the rights of all students are respected, including groups who lack the means to make their needs known, be it through immaturity or other circumstance.

I will exercise my professional judgment as independently as possible and be influenced neither by political pressures nor by factors such as the social standing of a student. I will not put personal biases or desire for advancement above my duty to students.

I recognize the special value of mathematics, but I also know that mathematics is not the only aim of education. I agree that all education should take place within an ethical framework and be relevant to the student's development. I will not provide pointless or harmful lessons.

I will ensure that students in my classes receive the information and support that they need to study mathematics and improve their knowledge. I will answer their questions truthfully and respectfully. If I cannot answer their questions, I will explain that and will seek additional help in finding valid answers.

I will encourage all students of differing abilities to participate in intellectually honest mathematics courses and will use a variety of strategies to help each student learn.

I will show respect for all those with whom I work and be ready to share my knowledge by teaching others what I know.

I will use my mathematics education and professional standing to improve the community in which I work. I will treat all student information in a professional manner. I will work to have a positive influence on authorities whose policies affect public education. I will oppose education policies that breach internationally accepted standards of human rights. I will strive to change laws that are contrary to students' interests and to my professional ethics.

AMERICAN ASSOCIATION FOR HEALTH EDUCATION

Code of Ethics for the Health Education Profession

Article I: Responsibility to the Public

Section 1: Health Educators support the right of individuals to make informed decisions regarding health, as long as such decisions pose no threat to the health of others.

Section 2: Health Educators encourage actions and social policies that support and facilitate the best balance of benefits over harm for all affected parties.

Section 3: Health Educators accurately communicate the potential benefits and consequences of the services and programs with which they are associated.

Section 4: Health Educators accept the responsibility to act on issues that can adversely affect the health of individuals, families, and communities.

Section 5: Health Educators are truthful about their qualifications and the limitations of their expertise and provide services consistent with their competencies.

Section 6: Health Educators protect the privacy and dignity of individuals.

Section 7: Health Educators actively involve individuals, groups, and communities in the entire educational process so that all aspects of the process are clearly understood by those who may be affected.

Section 8: Health Educators respect and acknowledge the rights of others to hold diverse values, attitudes, and opinions.

Section 9: Health Educators provide services equitably to all people.

Article II: Responsibility to the Profession

Section 1: Health Educators maintain, improve, and expand their professional competence through continued study and education; membership, participation, and leadership in professional organizations; and involvement in issues related to the health of the public.

Section 2: Health Educators model and encourage nondiscriminatory standards of behavior in their interactions with others.

Section 3: Health Educators encourage and accept responsible critical discourse to protect and enhance the profession.

Section 4: Health Educators contribute to the development of the profession by sharing the processes and outcomes of their work.

Section 5: Health Educators are aware of possible professional conflicts of interest, exercise integrity in conflict situations, and do not manipulate or violate the rights of others.

Section 6: Health Educators give appropriate recognition to others for their professional contributions and achievements.

Article III: Responsibility to Employers

Health Educators recognize the boundaries of their professional competence and are accountable for their professional activities and actions.

Section 1: Health Educators accurately represent their qualifications and the qualifications of others whom they recommend.

Section 2: Health Educators use appropriate standards, theories, and guidelines as criteria when carrying out their professional responsibilities.

Section 3: Health Educators accurately represent potential service and program outcomes to employers.

Section 4: Health Educators anticipate and disclose competing commitments, conflicts of interest, and endorsement of products.

Section 5: Health Educators openly communicate to employers, expectations of job-related assignments that conflict with their professional ethics.

Section 6: Health Educators maintain competence in their areas of professional practice.

Article IV: Responsibility in the Delivery of Health Education

Section 1: Health Educators are sensitive to social and cultural diversity and are in accord with the law, when planning and implementing programs.

Section 2: Health Educators are informed of the latest advances in theory, research, and practice, and use strategies and methods that are grounded in and contribute to development of professional standards, theories, guidelines, statistics, and experience.

Section 3: Health Educators are committed to rigorous evaluation of both program effectiveness and the methods used to achieve results.

Section 4: Health Educators empower individuals to adopt healthy lifestyles through informed choice rather than by coercion or intimidation.

Section 5: Health Educators communicate the potential outcomes of proposed services, strategies, and pending decisions to all individuals who will be affected.

Article V: Responsibility in Research and Evaluation

Section 1: Health Educators support principles and practices of research and evaluation that do no harm to individuals, groups, society, or the environment.

Section 2: Health Educators ensure that participation in research is voluntary and is based upon the informed consent of the participants.

Section 3: Health Educators respect the privacy, rights, and dignity of research participants, and honor commitments made to those participants.

Section 4: Health Educators treat all information obtained from participants as confidential unless otherwise required by law.

Section 5: Health Educators take credit, including authorship, only for work they have actually performed and give credit to the contributions of others.

Section 6: Health Educators who serve as research or evaluation consultants discuss their results only with those to whom they are providing service, unless maintaining such confidentiality would jeopardize the health or safety of others.

Section 7: Health Educators report the results of their research and evaluation objectively, accurately and in a timely fashion.

Article VI: Responsibility in Professional Preparation

Section 1: Health Educators select students for professional preparation programs based upon equal opportunity for all, and the individual's academic performance, abilities, and potential contribution to the profession and the public's health.

Section 2: Health Educators strive to make the educational environment and culture conducive to the health of all involved, and free from sexual harassment and all forms of discrimination.

Section 3: Health Educators involved in professional preparation and professional development engage in careful preparation; present material that is accurate, up-to-date, and timely; provide reasonable and timely feedback; state clear and reasonable expectations; and conduct fair assessments and evaluations of learners.

Section 4: Health Educators provide objective and accurate counseling to learners about career opportunities, development, and advancement, and assist learners to secure professional employment.

Section 5: Health Educators provide adequate supervision and meaningful opportunities for the professional development of learners.

PREPARED BY PROFESSIONAL ETHICS COMMITTEE

Approved by National Council for the Social Studies
Board of Directors, 1990, 2003

Revised Code of Ethics for the Social Studies Profession

Principle One: It is the ethical responsibility of social studies professionals to set forth, maintain, model, and safeguard standards of instructional competence suited to the achievement of the broad goals of the social studies.

Principle Two: It is the ethical responsibility of social studies professionals to provide to every student the knowledge, skills, experiences, and attitudes necessary to function as an effective participant in a democratic system.

Principle Three: It is the ethical responsibility of social studies professionals to foster the understanding and exercise the rights guaranteed under the Constitution of the United States and of the responsibilities implicit in those rights in an increasingly interdependent world.

Principle Four: It is the ethical responsibility of social studies professionals to cultivate and maintain an instructional environment in which the free contest of ideas is prized.

Principle Five: It is the ethical responsibility of social studies professionals to adhere to the highest standards of scholarship in the development, production, distribution, or use of social studies materials.

Principle Six: It is the ethical responsibility of social studies professionals to concern themselves with the conditions of the school and community with which they are associated.

Notes

CHAPTER 1

1. Nolte, Chester. 1978. *How to survive in teaching.* Chicago, IL: Teach'em Press.

2. Harris, Charles, Michael Pritchard, and Michael Rabins. 1995. Engineering ethcs: Concepts and cases. Illinois Institute of Technology, Codes of Ethics. http://ethics.iit.edu/codes/html.

3. Golnick, Donna. 2004. NCATE standard 1 and the new review process. http://www.ncate.org.

4. National Association for the Education of Young Children. 2005. Code of ethical conduct and statement of commitment. htttp://www.naeyc.org/about/positions.

5. Kidder, R. M. 1995. How good people make tough choices: Resolving the dilemmas of ethical living. New York: Fireside Publishers.

6. Textsheet.com Online, s.v. "Ethics," http://www.xplosive.sferahost.com/encyclopedia.

7. National Association for the Education of Young Children. 2005. Code of ethical conduct and statement of commitment. htttp://www.naeyc.org/about/positions.

8. Center for Creative Play. 1997. Guiding principles. Illinois Institute of Technology, Codes of Ethics. http://ethics.iit.edu/codes/html.

9. American Library Assoication.1981. Statement on professional ethics, 1981. Illinois Institute of Technology, Codes of Ethics. http://ethics.iit.edu/codes/html.

10. Rich, John Martin. 1984. Professional ethics in education. Springfield, IL: Charles C. Thomas Publishers, 122.

11. National Association for the Education of Young Children. 2005. Code of ethical conduct and statement of commitment. htttp://www.naeyc.org/about/positions.

12. National Education Association. 1975. Code of ethics of the education profession. http://www.nea.org.

13. Merriam-Webster Dictionary. 1997. s.v. "principle".

14. Council for Exceptional Children—Division of Early Childhood. 1999. Code of Ethics. www.gacec.org.

15. Rich, John Martin. 1984. *Professional ethics in education.* Springfield, IL: Charles C. Thomas Publishers, 11.

16. Rich, John Martin. 1984. *Professional ethics in education.* Springfield, IL: Charles C. Thomas Publishers, 9.

17. Luegenbiehl, Heinz C. 1991. Codes of ethics and the moral education of engineers. *Illinois Institute of Technology, Codes of Ethics.* http://ethics.iit.edu/codes/html.

18. Rich, John Martin. 1984. *Professional ethics in education.* Springfield, IL: Charles C. Thomas Publishers, 11.

19. Starratt, Robert J. 1991. Building an ethical school: A theory for practice in educational leadership. *Educational Administration Quarterly* 27: 185–202.

20. Carr, David. 2003. Moral educational implications of rival conceptions of education and the role of the teacher. *Journal of Moral Education* 32: 219–232.

21. Manos, Mary Ann. 2004. *Rumors, lies and whispers: Classroom crush or career catastrophe?* Westport, CT: Greenwood Publishers.

22. Baker, Robert. 1999. Codes of ethics: Some history. *Perspectives on the Professions, Illinois Institute of Technology, Codes of Ethics.* http://ethics.iit.edu/perspective.

23. Carr, David. 2003. Moral educational implications of rival conceptions of education and the role of the teacher. *Journal of Moral Education* 32: 219–232.

24. McKnight, Douglas. 2004. *An inquiry of NCATE's move into virtue ethics by way of dispositions (Is this what Aristotle meant?).* Mahwah, NJ: Lawrence Erlbaum Associates.

25. Belmonte, Dominic. 2003. *Teaching from the deep end: Succeeding with today's classroom challenges.* Thousand Oaks, CA: Corwin Press.

26. Haberman, Martin. 1995. *Star teachers of children in poverty.* West Lafayette, IN: Kappa Delta Pi.

27. Glasser, William. 1993. *The quality school teacher.* New York: HarperCollins Books.

28. Good, Thomas, and Jere Brophy. 2000. *Looking in classrooms.* New York: Addison Wesley Longman.

29. Bryk, Anthony, and Barbara Scheider. 2003. Trust in schools: A core resource for school reform. *Educational Leadership* 60 (March): 40–45.

30. Bergem, Trygve. 1990. The teacher as a moral agent. *Journal of Moral Education* 19 (May): 88–102.

31. Hirsch, E. D., Jr. 1993. *The schools we need and why we don't have them.* New York: Doubleday Publishers.

32. Mayor, John. 1965. *Accreditation in teacher education and its influence on higher education.* Washington, DC: National Commission on Accreditation.

33. State of Florida Department of Education. 2005. *State board of education, administrative rules code of ethics— principles of professional conduct for the education profession in Florida.* http://www.firn.edu/doe/rules.

34. State of New York Education Department. 2005. *Office of teaching initiatives teacher discipline.* http://higheded.nysed.gov/tcert.

35. Illinois State Board of Education. 2005. *History of the state certification board.* http://isbe.net/STCB/history.htm.

36. State of South Dakota. 2002. Senate Bill No. 31—An act to update references to the codes of ethics for teachers and administrators. 77th sess.

37. State of New Jersey. 2005. School ethics commission. http://www.state.nj.us/njded/ethics.

38. Alexander, Kern, and M. David Alexander. 2005. *American public school law.* Belmont, CA: Wadsworth Publishers.

39. Alexander, Kern, and M. David Alexander. 2005. *American public school law.* Belmont, CA: Wadsworth Publishers.

40. Alexander, Kern, and M. David Alexander. 2005. *American public school law.* Belmont, CA: Wadsworth Publishers.

41. U.S. Department of Education. 2005. Frequently asked questions. http://www.title2.org/faq.htm.

42. Mayor, John. 1965. *Accreditation in teacher education and its influence on higher education.* Washington, DC: National Commission on Accreditation.

43. McKnight, Douglas. 2004. *An inquiry of NCATE's move into virtue ethics by way of dispositions (Is this what Aristotle meant?).* Mahwah, N.J.: Lawrence Erlbaum Associates.

44. Golnick, Donna. 2004. NCATE standard 1 and the new review process. http://www.ncate.org.

45. Golnick, Donna. 2004. NCATE standard 1 and the new review process. http://www.ncate.org.

CHAPTER 2

1. Peterson, P. E., and M. West. 2003. *No child left behind?* Washington, DC: Brookings Institution Press.

2. Garcia by Garcia v. Miera, U.S. Court of Appeals, 1987. 817 F. 2nd 650.

3. Parker Palmer. 1998. *The courage to teach.* San Francisco: Jossey-Bass Publishing.

4. Doe v. Berkley County School District, U.S. District Court for the District of South Carolina, Charleston Division, 989 F. Supp. 768: 1997 U.S. Dist. Lexis 21100.

5. Imber, Michael, and Tyll Van Geel. 2005. *A teacher's guide to education law.* 3rd ed. Mahwah, NJ: Lawrence Erlbaum Publishers.

6. Fielder v. Board of Education, 346 F.Supp. 722, Nebr. (1972).

7. Garber v. Central High School, 295 N.Y.S. 2d 850 (1937).

8. Graham v. Charleston City School Bd., 204 S.E. 2d 384, S.C. (1974).

9. Lilienthal v. San Leandro Unified School District, 293 P.2d 889 (Calif. 1956).

10. Grayned v. Rockford, 408 U.S. 104 (1972).

11. Dailey v. Los Angeles Unified School District, 2 Cal. 3d 741, 87 Cal. Rptr. 376, 470 P.2d 360 (1970).

12. Hoyem v. Manhattan Beach School District, 585 p.2d 851 (Cal 1978).

13. Vaughn v. Orleans Parish School Board, 802 So. 2nd 967 (La. Ct. App. 2001).

14. Kelly, Evelyn. 1998. *Legal basics: A handbook for educators.* Bloomington, IN: Phi Delta Kappa Educational Foundation.

15. Goss v. Lopez, 419 U.S. 565 (1975).

16. Daily v. Board of Education of Morrill County School District No.62-0063, 256 Neb. 73, 588 N.W. 2d 813 (1999).

17. Sylvester v. Cancinne, 664 So. 2d 1259 (La. App. 1st Cir.1995).

18. Gerkes v. Deathe, 832 F.Supp. 1450 (W.D. Okla. 1993).

19. Ingraham v. Wright, 430 U.S. 651 (1977).

20. Moore v. Willis Independent School District, 248 F3d 1145 (5th Cir.2000).

21. U.S. v. Coffeeville Consolidated School District, 513 F. 2d 244, Miss., 5CA (1975).

22. Sheehan v. St. Peter's Catholic School, 291 Minn. 1 188 N.W.2d 868 (1971).

23. Gorton v. Doty, 69 P. 2d 136, Ida. (1937).

24. Hanson v. Reedley Jt. School District 111, P.2d 415, California (1941).

25. American Federation of Teachers. 2005. Substitute care: Teachers, paras forced to take on medical care of chronically ill students. *American Teacher* 90 (November): 20.

26. Barrett v. Unified School District No. 259, 32 P.3d 1156 (Kan. 2001).

27. Davis v. Gonzales, 931 S.W. 2nd 15 (Tex. App.-Corpus Christi 1996).

28. Kimberly S.M. v. Bradford Central School, 649 N.Y.S. 2d 588 (A.D. 4th Dept. 1996).

29. Imber, Michael, and Tyll Van Geel. 2005. *A teacher's guide to education law.* 3rd ed. Mahwah, NJ: Lawrence Erlbaum Publishers.

30. Owasso Independent School Dist. No. I-0111 v. Falvo 534 U.S. 426 (2002).

31. American Association of University Women. 2001. *Hostile hallways: The AAUW survey on sexual harassment in America's schools.* Washington, DC: American Association of University Women.

32. Metropolitan Life Insurance Company. 1999. *American teacher, 1999: Violence in America's public schools: Five years later.* New York: Metropolitan Life Insurance Company.

33. Shakesshaft, Carol, and Audrey Cohan. 1995. Sexual abuse of students by school personnel. *Phi Delta Kappan* 76 (March): 512–520.

34. American Association of University Women. 2001. *Hostile hallways: The AAUW survey on sexual harassment in America's schools.* Washington, DC: American Association of University Women.

35. Lee, Valarie, Robert Croninger, Eleanor Linn, and Xianglei Chen. 1996. The culture of sexual harassment in secondary schools. *American Educational Research Journal* 33 (Summer): 338–417.

36. Sandler, Bernice. 2001. *Educator's guide to controlling sexual harassment.* Washington, DC: Thompson Publishing.

37. Ancel, Glink, Diamond, Bush, DiCianni, and Rolek. 1998. Teacher/sexual harassment. *Education Law Report* No.1 (November): 1–12.

38. Bureau of Justice Statistics. 2001. *National crime victimization survey.* Washington, DC: U.S. Department of Justice.

CHAPTER 3

1. National Association of Secondary School Principals. 2005. Legal clips: Recent developments in school law. http://www.principals.org/s_nassp.

2. Lifton v. Board of Education of Chicago, 416 F3d 571 2005 Lexis 14933.

3. U.S. Code 1401 (11).

4. Canter, Lee. 1992. *Assertive discipline.* Santa Monica, CA: Canter and Associates.

5. Canter, Lee. 1992. *Assertive discipline.* Santa Monica, CA: Canter and Associates.

6. Nolte, Chester. 1971. *School law in action: 101 key decisions with guidelines for school administrators,* West Nyack, NY: Parker Publishing.

7. Braun, Brian A. 2004. Illinois school law survey. Springfield, IL: Illinois Association of School Boards.

8. National Center for Education Statistics. 2001. Teacher victimization at school. http://www.nces.ed.gov/pubs2004/crime.

9. Kelly, Evelyn. 1998. *Legal basics: A handbook for educators.* Bloomington, IN: Phi Delta Kappa Educational Foundation.

10. Kelly, Evelyn. 1998. *Legal basics: A handbook for educators.* Bloomington, IN: Phi Delta Kappa Educational Foundation.

11. Florida State Statutes (FS 231.06, 1995).

12. Braun, Brian A. 2004. Illinois school law survey. Springfield, IL: Illinois Association of School Boards.

13. Lovern v. Edwards, 190 F.3d 648 (4th Cir.1999).

14. Huxten v Villasenor, 798 S. 2d (La. Ct. App. 2001).

15. U.S. Department of Education. 2005. The elementary and secondary education act—No Child Left Behind Act of 2001. http://www.ed.gov/policy/elsec/leg.

16. Killian, Johnny. 1979. The constitution of the United States. Washington, DC: U.S. Government Printing Office.

17. Family Educational Rights and Privacy Act, 20 U.S.C. §1232g; 34 CFR Part 99. http://www.ed.gov/policy/gen/guid/fpco/ferpa.html.

18. Imber, Michael, and Tyll Van Geel. 2005. A teacher's guide to education law. 3rd ed. Mahwah, NJ: Lawrence Erlbaum Publishers.

19. Crochiere v. Board of Education of the Town of Enfield et al., 227 Conn. 333 630 A.2d 1027 (1993).

20. Imber, Michael, and Tyll Van Geel. 2005. A teacher's guide to education law. 3rd ed. Mahwah, NJ: Lawrence Erlbaum Publishers.

21. Sauls and Sauls et.al. v. Pierce County School District et al., 399 F. 3d 1279 2005 U.S. App. Lexis 2043.

22. Braun, Brian A. 2004. Illinois school law survey. Springfield, IL: Illinois Association of School Boards.

23. Kelly, Evelyn. 1998. *Legal basics: A handbook for educators.* Bloomington, IN: Phi Delta Kappa Educational Foundation.

24. Krizek v. Cicero-Stickney Township High School District No. 201, 713 F. Supp 1131 (N.D. ILL.1989).

25. Leebaert v. Harrington, 332 F. 3d 134 (2003).

26. Kelly, Evelyn. 1998. *Legal basics: A handbook for educators.* Bloomington, IN: Phi Delta Kappa Educational Foundation.

27. Nolte, Chester. 1978. *How to survive in teaching.* Chicago, IL: Teach'em Press.

28. Nolte, Chester. 1978. *How to survive in teaching.* Chicago, IL: Teach'em Press.

29. Palmer v. Board of Education of Chicago, 603 F. 2d. 1271 (7th Cir. 1979).

30. Osborne, Allan. 2002. Proving that you have provided a FAPE under IDEA. *ELA Notes* (Winter 2002).

31. Osborne, Allan. 2002. Proving that you have provided a FAPE under IDEA. *ELA Notes* (Winter 2002).

32. Protection of Pupils Act, Section 439 of the General Education Provisions Act (20 U.S.C.A. 1232h) Goals 2000 Educate America Act.

CHAPTER 4

1. Imber, Michael, and Tyll Van Geel. 2005. *A teacher's guide to education law.* 3rd ed. Mahwah, NJ: Lawrence Erlbaum Publishers.

2. LaMorte, Michael. 2002. *School law: Cases and concepts.* Boston: Allyn & Bacon.

3. Sullivan v. Meade County Indep. School Dist., 530 F2d. 799 (S. Dak., 1976).

4. Hendrie, Caroline. 1998. Passing the trash by school district frees sexual predators to hunt again. *Education Week* (December 9): 16–17.

5. Toney v. Fairbanks North Star Borough School District, 881 P.2d 1112 (1994).

6. Hutton, Tom. 2003. "Vermont Dept. of Education plans to post information on teacher disciplinary cases on its Web site." Legal Clips, National School Boards Association (October).

7. Nolte, Chester. 1978. *How to survive in teaching.* Chicago: Teach'em Press.

8. Alexander, Kern, and M. David Alexander. 2005. *American public school law.* Belmont, CA: Wadsworth Publishers.

9. Negrich v. Dade County Board of Education, 143 So.2d 498 U.S. 836 (1974).

10. Alexander, Kern, and M. David Alexander. 2005. *American public school law.* Belmont, CA: Wadsworth Publishers.

11. Knox County Education Association v. Knox County Board of Education, 158 F.3d. 361 (6th Cir. 1998).

12. Nolte, Chester. 1978. *How to survive in teaching.* Chicago: Teach'em Press.

13. Snider v. Kit Carson School District R-1 in Cheyenne County, 166 Colo. 180 442 P2d. 429 (1968).

14. Kelly, Evelyn. 1998. *Legal basics: A handbook for educators.* Bloomington, IN: Phi Delta Kappa Educational Foundation.

15. Imber, Michael, and Tyll Van Geel. 2005. *A teacher's guide to education law.* 3rd ed. Mahwah, NJ: Lawrence Erlbaum Publishers.

16. Black, Henry. 1979. *Black's law dictionary.* St. Paul, MN: West Publishing.

17. Garcia by Garcia v. Miera, U.S. Court of Appeals, 1987. 817 F. 2nd 650.

18. Board of Regents of State College v. Roth, 408 U.S. 564 (1972).

19. Imber, Michael, and Tyll Van Geel. 2005. *A teacher's guide to education law.* 3rd ed. Mahwah, NJ: Lawrence Erlbaum Publishers.

20. East Hartford Education Association v. Board of Education of the Town of East Hartford, 562 F 2d. 838 (1977).

21. Chicago Teachers Union Local No. 1 v. Hudson, 475 U.S. 292 (1986).

22. Garland Independent School District v. Texas State Teacher's Association, 777 F 2d. (1946).

23. Alexander, Kern, and M. David Alexander. 2005. *American public school law.* Belmont, CA: Wadsworth Publishers.

24. Board of Regents of State College v. Roth, 408 U.S. 564 (1972).

25. Evens v. Superior Court of Los Angeles County, 77 Cal. App. 4th (1999).

26. Rolando v. School Directors, 358 N.E. 2d 945. Ill (1976).

27. George, Paul, and William Alexander. *The exemplary middle school.* Belmont, CA: Wadsworth/Thompson Learning.

28. Millikan v. Board of Directors of Everett School District, 611 P. 2d 414 (Wash. 1980).

29. Henderson v. Members of Benton County Board of Education, C.A. No. W1999-00247-COA-R3-CV, Tenn. App. (2000).

30. Moore v. Order of Minor Conventuals, 164 F. Supp. 711 (N.C. 1958).

31. Alexander, Kern, and M. David Alexander. 2005. *American public school law.* Belmont, CA: Wadsworth Publishers.

32. U.S. Department of Education. (2003). No Child Left Behind: A toolkit for teachers. http://www.ed.gov/teachers/nclbguide.

33. Illinois State Board of Education. 2003. State superintendent of education starts process for revoking two North Greene educator's licenses. http://www.isbe.net/news/2003.

34. Illinois State Board of Education. 2003. State superintendent of education starts process for revoking two North Greene educator's licenses. http://www.isbe.net/news/2003.

35. National Education Association. 2003. High-stakes tests spawn high-stakes lawsuits: Teachers fired, sued for revealing test questions, while a testing company agrees to pay $12 million for faulty scoring. *NEA TODAY* (May). http://www.nea.org/neatoday/0305/rights.html.

36. U.S. Equal Employment Opportunity Commission. Federal equal employment opportunity laws. http://www.eeoc.gov/abouteeo/overview_laws.html.

37. National Association of State Boards of Education. 2005. Retaliation for protesting unequal treatment under title IX. *Legal Briefs* (May).

38. Manos, Mary Ann. 2004. *Rumors, lies and whispers: Classroom crush or career catastrophe?* Westport, CT: Greenwood Publishers.

39. Tweedall V. Fritz, U.S. District Court of the Southern District of Indiana, Evansville Division, 987 F. Supp. 1126; 1997 U.S. Lexis 207066; 77 Fair Empl. Pra. Cas. (BNA) 1777.

40. Strauss, Susan. 1992. *Sexual harassment and teens.* Minneapolis.: Free Spirit, 1992.

41. Hendrie, Caroline. 1988. Passing the trash by school district frees sexual predators to hunt again. *Education Week* (December 9), 16–17.

CHAPTER 5

1. Carr, David. 2003. Moral educational implications of rival conceptions of education and the role of the teacher. *Journal of Moral Education* 32: 219–232.

2. Manos, Mary Ann. 2004. *Rumors, lies and whispers: Classroom crush or career catastrophe?* Westport, CT: Greenwood Publishers.

3. Morrison v. State Board of Education, 461 P.2d 375 (Cal. 1969).

4. Dubuclet v. Home Insurance Co., 660 So. 2d 67 (La. Ct. App.1995).

5. Dubuclet v. Home Insurance Co., 660 So. 2d 67 (La. Ct. App.1995).

6. Alexander, Kern, and M. David Alexander. 2005. *American public school law.* Belmont, CA: Wadsworth Publishers.

7. Pickering v. Board of Education, 391 U.S. 563 88 S.Ct. 1731, 20 L.Ed 811 (1968).

8. Urofsky v. Gilmore, 216 F.3d 401 (4th Cir. 2000).

9. Miles v. Denver Public Schools, 944 F 2d 773 (10th Cir. 1991).

10. Wheeler v. Natale, 178 F. Supp. 2d 407 (S.D.N.Y. 2001).

11. Downs v. Los Angeles Unified School Dist., 228 F.3d 1003 (9th Cir. 2000).

12. California Teachers Association v. Governing Board of San Diego Unified School District, 53 Cal. Reptr. 2d 474 (Cal. App. 4th Dist. 1996).

13. Love v. City of Chicago Board of Education, 241 F. 3d 564 (7th Cir. 2001).

14. Waters v. Churchill, 511 U.S. 661 (1994).

15. LaMorte, Michael. 2002 *School law: Cases and concepts.* Boston: Allyn & Bacon.

16. Hatch Act (5 U.S.C. subsection 1501–1508), Office of Special Counsel. http://www.osc.gov/ha_state.htm.

17. LaMorte, Michael. 2002 *School law: Cases and concepts.* Boston: Allyn & Bacon.

18. Imber, Michael, and Tyll Van Geel. 2005. A teacher's guide to education law. 3rd ed. Mahwah, NJ: Lawrence Erlbaum Publishers.

19. LaMorte, Michael. 2002 *School law: Cases and concepts.* Boston: Allyn & Bacon, p. 259.

20. Imber, Michael, and Tyll Van Geel. 2005. *A teacher's guide to education law.* 3rd ed. Mahwah, NJ: Lawrence Erlbaum Publishers.

21. School Commissioners of Westerly v. Westerly Teachers Association, 299, 2d 441 (R.I. 1973).

Index

About the Author and Contributors

AUTHOR

Mary Ann Manos, PhD, is a 30-year veteran of the classroom. Dr. Manos holds a Ph.D. in Curriculum and Instruction from the University of Texas at Austin, Texas. She is a 2000 National Board for Professional Teaching Standards certified teacher in Early Adolescent English/Language Arts. She has taught elementary school through college level, in public and private settings.

Dr. Manos is the author of two professional books and several articles. She is an Associate Professor in Teacher Education at Bradley University, in Peoria, IL. Her work at the university level includes teaching middle school methods and education foundation courses, as well as courses on gifted education. She served for four years as the Director of the Bradley University Institute for Gifted and Talented Youth. Dr. Manos also works with the International Study Abroad programs at Bradley.

CONTRIBUTORS

Dr. Shari Britner is an assistant professor at Bradley University. Her research and publications focus on attitudes and motivations in science, particularly self-efficacy; inquiry-oriented science pedagogy, and equity issues in science and science education. She teaches elementary science education, supervises student teachers, and is the Professional Development School Site Coordinator for a large urban middle school. She previously taught elementary and middle school science for 17 years. She earned National Board Teacher certification in 1994.

Dr. Cindy Brubaker is a registered nurse and an Assistant Professor of Nursing at Bradley University. Her research interest include the measurement of ethical caring within clinical encounters between student nurses and patients and the teaching of ethical caring within nursing education.

Sandra Holman, J.D., has been employed since 1985 by the Illinois Education Association-NEA, with a focus on education and labor/employment issues from an employee/union perspective. Ms. Holman is a graduate of Washington University, St. Louis (B.A. 1973) and Boston University School of Law (J.D. 1976).

Ms. Holman is licensed to practice law in both Illinois (1976) and Missouri (1982) and focuses on labor and employment law.

Dr. Victoria Huffman is an Assistant Professor of Teacher Education at Bradley University. Her research interests include the measurement of ethical caring as demonstrated in the pedagogical practices of student teachers and the teaching of ethical caring within teacher preparation.

Dr. Sherrie Pardiek is an Assistant Professor of Elementary Education at Bradley University, where she has held a variety of teaching and supervising positions since 1989. For several years prior to joining the university, Dr. Pardiek taught in public schools at the preschool, elementary, and middle school levels.

Dr. Jenny Tripses teaches in the Educational Leadership program at Bradley University. She has 17 years' experience teaching grades K–3, adult education, and high school at-risk students. For nine years, she was an elementary school principal. For the past seven years, Dr. Tripses has taught graduate students preparing to become principals. She consults with local school teachers on assessment and curriculum development.

Lisa Uphoff is a Field Service Director for the Illinois Federation of Teachers. Prior to her employment with the IFT, she taught high school social studies for 11 years in Farmington, IL. Alongside her teaching duties, Lisa headed the history department, coached volleyball and scholastic bowl, sponsored the National Honor Society, served as a class sponsor, and served as the president of her local union for three and a half years. She resides in Peoria, IL.